The Freedom to Lie : A Debate about Democracy

THE FREEDOM TO LIE
A Debate about Democracy

John Swan *and* Noel Peattie

*An enlargement of the 1988 debate,
"Two Views of Intellectual Freedom,"
sponsored by the Social Responsibilities Round Table
and the Intellectual Freedom Round Table
of the American Library Association
at their Annual Conference in New Orleans*

WITH ANNOTATED BIBLIOGRAPHIES
BY BOTH PARTICIPANTS

Foreword by Robert Franklin

McFarland & Company, Inc., Publishers
Jefferson, North Carolina, and London

British Library Cataloguing-in-Publication data available

Library of Congress Cataloguing-in-Publication Data

Swan, John.
  The freedom to lie.

  "An enlargement of the 1988 debate, 'Two views of
intellectual freedom,' sponsored by the Social Responsibilities Round Table and the Intellectual Freedom
Round Table of the American Library Association at
their Annual Conference in New Orleans."
  "With annotated bibliographies by both participants."
  1. Libraries — Censorship — Congresses. 2. Freedom
of Information — Congresses. I. Peattie, Noel.
II. American Library Association. Social Responsibilities Round Table. III. American Library Association.
Intellectual Freedom Round Table. IV. Title.
Z711.4.S9 1989   025.2′13   89-45000

ISBN 0-89950-409-4 (lib. bdg. : 50# alk. paper) ∞

Printed in the United States of America.

McFarland & Company, Inc., Publishers
  Box 611, Jefferson, North Carolina 28640

To
Dorothy M. Broderick
and
E.J. Josey

Two Disclaimers

John Swan and Noel Peattie

J.S.: Although two American Library Association round tables, one devoted to Social Responsibilities and the other to Intellectual Freedom, were supportive in sponsoring the original debate, and although my position was originally identified in a general way with that of the latter round table, I hereby serve notice that my contributions to that event and to this book do not in any way carry the authority of official policy. I have been privileged to receive much enlightenment and support from my colleagues on the Intellectual Freedom Round Table, as well as from the Office for Intellectual Freedom and other American Library Association bodies; however, any pandering to liars and cheats, any neglect and or suppression of truth-tellers, the oppressed, and good persons that one detects in my arguments, should be charged to me personally rather than these valuable and socially progressive organizations.

N.P.: Some of the text under my name has been seen in a draft version by some members of the American Library Association's Social Responsibilities Round Table. No attempt has been made to get official endorsement from SRRT's Action Council or from its membership. My views do not therefore necessarily coincide with SRRT policy, or with the views of any members, and I take sole responsibility for the opinions here expressed. It follows that I have made no attempt to be "politically correct," since that phrase is indefinable and refers only to the state of mind of its user. I once had a button that said "POLITICALLY CORRECT," but I gave it away to a friend who was going to Germany; the woman who made the buttons told me later that she wasn't making them any more.

Acknowledgments

Noel Peattie and *John Swan*

N.P.: Earlier versions of "Truth, Libraries, and Revolution," the substance of my debate presentation in New Orleans in 1988, have been read and criticized by the following scholars, whom the author especially desires to thank my brother Professor Mark Peattie, Department of History, University of Massachusetts, Boston; Professor Whitney Gordon, Department of Sociology, Ball State University, Muncie, Indiana; and Professor John Malcolm, Department of Philosophy, University of California, Davis.

Special thanks also go to librarians Sanford Berman, Hennepin County Library, Edina, Minnesota; Jackie Eubanks, Brooklyn College Library; Zoia Horn, Data Center, Oakland, California; Linda Pierce, Anchorage Public Library, Alaska; and Thomas McFadden, University of California, Davis.

The criticisms of professors Gordon and Malcolm, and Librarian McFadden, have been especially trenchant. A special mention must go to my distinguished antagonist, Librarian John C. Swan, of Bennington College, Vermont, whose riposte to my thrust was a chief stimulus in rewriting my entire text; E.J. Josey and Corinne Nyquist, who supplied information on the South Africa boycott movement; and my publisher, Robert Franklin, who persuaded me to write, and rewrite, an essay the length of a master's thesis in six months.

J.S.: Heartfelt thanks to the people at McFarland, for initiating, prodding, clarifying, insisting, and tolerating; to our original debate audience (with particular tributes to Eric Moon, Gordon Conable, and Beth Rile) who were a lot better show than we were;

to John Berry and *Library Journal* for so freely granting the right to reprint my article "Untruth or Consequences"; to David Budbill, for being steadfast and eloquent in the face of the censorship of his work; to my wife Susan, who has listened to a lot of raving with characteristic intelligence; and to Noel Peattie, who has persisted in asking important questions, and who has responded to much intemperate negativity with grace and generosity of spirit.

Table of Contents

The Dolphins: A Foreword

(by Robert Franklin)

One is grateful for the invitation to write about dolphins. Anywhere is a good place to, but here is even better. Dolphins are the right things to write about when, precisely, freedom of information and social responsibility are up.

Readers who do not skip forewords in order to plunge into the main meat but who maintain an orderly approach to books and sentences may at this point wonder, now, ... dolphins? Nothing else in this Swan and Peattie book seems to have anything to do with them. But can you not see them, there! arcing over the bow wave, leading us, indefatigable, ancient?

First, the amenities. This is a guest foreword to a book by Noel Peattie and John Swan that first bloomed in New Orleans in 1988 as a "debate" sponsored by two praiseworthy organs of the American Library Association, the Social Responsibilities Round Table and the Intellectual Freedom Round Table. The two agreed to stage a duel in the arena of free speech. Each chose a noble champion; not coincidentally, each champion had slain his most recent dragon on the plains of McCalden.*

In the event, pennants of prose whipped briskly, nor was the droll aside unheard. We audience were swept to a high plane uncharacteristic of ALA conferences. About 130 were in the room; the loser of the debate was to take the winner to dinner.

Mr. Peattie was broadminded and socially responsible. He

---

*David McCalden, the Holocaust-didn't-happen fellow who ran afoul of the California Library Association over matters of free speech; many words are devoted to him passim in the pages to follow.

embraced nearly all that humankind might express. Nearly all; the rest, it would be irresponsible to embrace.

Mr. Swan was free in speech. All that can be said, may be. (Perhaps he even argued *should* be.)

In many ways the social view is easiest to argue. One can find so many damnable acts to indict. One can be, so indicting, liked or elected or left with children safely. Hating hatred sounds good to most.

The absolutist view, oft alone, gazes from a high crag. Missteps, loose rocks; holding all speech to be free one might come to wish one were a spirit, where the very air buoyed one and shifting grounds didn't threaten. To the absolutist, every evil is one's guest; every vile possibility, entertained. (This is, remember, speech we speak of, not actions.) The free speech advocate can be painted a monster easily, and the I-draw-the-line-here, a hero.

Yet at the end the audience voted 76 for Swan, the eloquent knight for IFRT, and 26 for Peattie, the intellectual SRRT man. A further and coincidental 26 voted to abstain (this *was* an ALA event), clearly the most interesting tally. Librarians, much like just people, love good. This final 26 were perhaps proto–Swanians who could not shake their vision of the muck and ugliness implicit in his position — a 26 who, for socially responsible reasons, could not confess their permissiveness. Else, those who were native Peattites, his sharp and bright speech would surely have won.

In the present book are their set-pieces in this ersatz debate (the two opposed, but with polished speeches; a measure of give-and-take, or assertion and rebuttal, glimmered in the audience questions windup, but a debate verily it was not), plus another apropos essay or two each. Each has furthermore offered a timely and germane appendix and an annotated bibliography at the back.

Why dolphins? Let us not answer until we have described the book at hand in more depth.

Through the fall of 1988 and into 1989 a lively correspondence developed with the freely speaking messrs. Swan and Peattie in which I, the third corner, played foil and conduit.

During this time the real world gave us continuously a fresh supply of dilemmas of free speech against which to measure our feelings. Among the most poignant was that brought back to mind by the death February 2 of Oliver W. Sipple, a former marine who thwarted an attempt to assassinate President Gerald R. Ford in September 1975. In heralding him as a hero, and reporting numerous commendations, the media identified him as a homosexual who frequented San Francisco's gay bars. This publicity caused great suffering, not least of which was alienation from his family whom he had never told.

Mr. Sipple sued seven newspapers and 50 executives of those newspapers, saying the disclosure had caused him "great mental anguish, embarrassment and humiliation." "My sexuality is a part of my private life and has no bearing on my response to the act of a person seeking to take the life of another," he said upon announcing the suit. The suit was dismissed by the California Supreme Court in 1984, at least in part on the grounds that his sexual orientation had been known to hundreds of people before the news accounts.

Another issue arose in February that in one's innermost bones and darker moments could seem cataclysmic. The Ayatollah Khomeini's public offer to pay millions for the murder of novelist Salman Rushdie for blaspheming Islam is taken seriously by the entire world. As humanity enters the cusp of a millennium, as the magical year "2000" looms like a stone tribal god over the scrabbling obeisances of religious zealots, the freedom to lie, to create or deny, to propound or reserve, will predictably ever more be feverishly tested. (Both debaters remark herein on the Rushdie affair.)

On a more classical note: Knowing the book was underway and that almost no one has managed to deal with this topic without reference to the august John Stuart Mill, Eric Moon happed upon and sent along a paragraph from *On Liberty* that neither Swan nor Peattie has favored, yet which seems even more definitive than those passages the debaters did use:

> Strange it is, that men should admit the validity of the arguments for free discussion, but object to their being "pushed to an extreme"; not seeing that unless the reasons are good for an extreme case, they are not good for any case. Strange that they should imagine that they are not assuming infallibility, when they acknowledge that there should be free discussion on all subjects which can possibly be *doubtful,* but think that some particular principle or doctrine should be forbidden to be questioned because it is *so certain,* that is, because *they are certain* that it is certain. To call any proposition certain, while there is anyone who would deny its certainty if permitted, but who is not permitted, is to assume that we ourselves, and those who agree with us, are the judges of certainty, and judges without hearing the other side.

The letters flowing between Winters, Bennington and Jefferson over the winter were a positive blossoming of sociability and responsiveness. The book had to be more than just the New Orleans debates or it would be too small and the publisher couldn't put a price on it. It had to be self-aware (why should the one knock the other's point, when it had been withdrawn in a more recent revision), but not trapped in an Escher-like infinite regression of revision and counter-revision. And it had to have a good title.

Many titles were tendered — "The Fascist in the Fishbowl" was, for instance, an early Peattie entry, but his swallower eel *(Saccopharynx harrisoni)* imagery wound up being pulled from the final version. The deleted passage, heavy of metaphor, ran something like this: The god of an ocean-world invited all fish to come live there freely. O.k., said *harrisoni,* who, upon arrival, set about devouring all the other fish; when the panthalassic deity protested, the fish said, "too late, you can't stop me," gulping down the sea-god, gulp, gulp, gulp. For me, in the front row, these three Peattie stage gulps were a theatrical high point.

With his "The Freedom to Lie" already on the table, Swan nevertheless tested with "Dangerous Freedom: Librarians in the Age of (Dis)Information." The publisher rebutted that "Lie" hits higher on the carnival sledgehammer-clanger of human emotion than "Danger," a distancing Latinism that meant first in English, merely, the extent of one's holdings that are exposed to risks: "lie," to the contrary, lies at the language's Germanic hearth-and-crib heart.

Various turns on "Between Truth and Freedom" yielded three-way agreement that, essentially, there was no "between." Perhaps eyeing the Vermont winter, John called it the slushiest of prepositions. A better concept was "Truth and Freedom Really Do Merge," a phrase buried in a letter from Noel that otherwise explicated the "between" as embracing the dilemma of a librarian forced to choose: This book is claptrap but do the people need access. . .? As we three drifted again toward "The Freedom to Lie," a go at "Liars and Librarians" arose; this one added alliteration to titular virtues, but underrepresented the scope of the book by seeming to limit it to librarians.

"Two Views of Intellectual Freedom," a phrase that bannered the original ALA debate, seemed unrevealing. "Truth versus Access," "Access and Advocacy" (highbrow assonance, demurred the publisher), and "Librarians and the Democratic Dilemma" all were considered. Finally the trio concluded that "we need to lie our way out of the library science ghetto," as wry John put it, and chose what became the published version.

No title was correct. "A Debate about Democracy," for instance: Citizenry in and out of the library and information profession tend seldom to be reminded what narrow point the Greek word "democracy" is making, among the "-cracies." Certainly the patriots of 1789 had no truck with "democracy" (one can imagine the John Adams lip curling). Their thing was truly the public thing, the *res publica*, the "republic," the government of laws. There is no "democracy" in the Constitution. The reader is free to doubt that what is herein known to be not a debate is about democracy either.

"The Freedom to Lie": well of course the phrase should not be taken to imply that the authors or publisher believe that humans, or Americans, or other people have such a freedom. Law in the United States leans evermore toward discovering lie, and limiting our right to utter it. Purveyors of toothpaste and tobacco are effectively enjoined; our own bodies—pupils, cheek color, manner of hands—betray our lies, and limit them.

Still evolving, the human aptitude for lying seems clearly biological. As creatures evolved toward more "control" of their environment (actually they'd merely developed more flexibility toward it), imposing order upon the reality observed became feasible and desirable. (Or, roughly equally likely, desirable and feasible: cause and effect are often indistinguishable in evolution.) If the environment is another word for the "truth," the native manipulations of humans are, then, "lies." To control is to lie, simplistically put. The "lie" was made a Homosapient crime surely many millennia after the first falsity.

And so what are lies now? Well, who can tell? Neither debater nor reader knows. Take physicists. They are unsure what "reality" is or what its constituents are. (Nonphysicists, one may be assured, are equally unsure.) What can knowledge then mean? The exhilarating fact is, each year or two, we know less! That is, we have discovered so many more variables (that we cannot "control," to use laboratory terminology), cross-correspondences, unrepeatable (the lab term) occurrences, that even with "breakthroughs" both subatomic and pangalactic, we have ever less of a basis for drawing conclusions. So, what *is* the creation of a lie? (Forget about *why* do it; the cause-and-effect here seems clearly to be: capacity produces ability produces exercise thereof; invention has been and will always be a mother of necessity.)

One might say that lies are "different" realities for a relatively few people to sample for a relatively limited period of time. Who can argue that this is not useful to Biology? Chickens swallow gravel to help digestion. The constant crunch-testing of contending realities will insure that the testing capability, probably even the mechanism, is passed down over the millions. Both sides in the present debate can certainly agree to this. "The price of liberty eternal vigilance" is a more recent, a Latin, way of citing this crunch-testing necessity.

So, what about lying? Forget it, it's not a topic. Your freedom to tell lies certainly is, but lying itself has no description. (O.k., it *is* a "topic" but just to the extent one can easily name things that it is *not:* anti–God, immoral, life-threatening, non-survival-valueist, aberrational, abnormal, exotic, unusual, or worth noting. It's more like breathing and blinking.) In the title of this book, it is "Freedom" that has the emphasis.

In the earliest human communities, where all knew the wealth of all, and health too, it may be presumed that the performances of all — teachers, warriors, baby-tenders, healers, hunters, story-tellers — were known (and probably rated). The retired were welded to their reputations. Stealing was punished by laughter and stares; who would blatantly commit such foolery before the very eyes of "the entire world"? Lying could only have been even less significant or prevalent. Murder, rampage, injury: these certainly were practiced 40,000 years ago as they are now, but one may doubt, for instance, that the jealous slayer of long ago would pretend another had done it.

In the early community of my fantasy you could lose your integrity quickly by claiming a coup or a kill you did not make, an accuracy you did not possess, a courage, a skill, a love for another you did not have. The chances that the small band of humanity around you would accept your false version would be remote. Put another way, the closeness they would feel for you, the since-a-baby knowledge they'd have of your behavior and nervous system and eating habits, the memories they would have of your parents and grandparents, the facts they would have of your performance — all this would enable the most unconscious of them to know, right off, your veracity. By smell alone and in the first few milliseconds, wouldn't surprise me. In this way they were no doubt closer to the dolphins than we are now. Integrity was everything. It isn't now.

And the dolphins? They have pushed both freedom of information and social responsibility to the greatest possible extent. Dolphins (and whales)—forgiving of human torment, selfless imitators of the best lines, curves, arcs in art—were not on that salvaging ark with Noah; had it perished, they would still have carried the best that Earth had to offer. With their lungs and vestigial hips and fingers reminding that they too had tried land, and maybe lies, and went back to the sea.

Dolphins have an astoundingly powerful sonar-like capacity. Somewhat in the manner of bats, they bounce sound off objects and passages, and easily determine prey or way. But like the apparatus of modern labs, their sound can pass all the way through flesh, and also partway through, before bouncing back. Dolphins diagnose physical status—not just illness—instantly, in any swimming thing. A little tension, intestinal gas, kidney stone, lump in the throat, the dolphins "ping"—politely one may be sure—and perceive all. If you could posit the existence of lies in dolphins you would know they would all be transparent. No dissembler, the cetacean. Whatever might be *like* lies, is, among these huge-brains (bigger than humans'), probably art. (Dolphins talk and sing as richly as men and women.) They are "free" to "lie" but cannot.

But, still, why has the dolphin flopped upon the dry land of Swan and Peattie debate? So what, this precious animal? For one thing, the dolphin may reassure the philosophers of human evolution that the ever greater tendency toward all-knowledge about everyone need not turn out bad. Were we delphinate, we might be assured that truth and transparency will not bring us to dark ends, and low lives.

But there is a further fact to learn. The sound-wave generating capacity of dolphins is more powerful than you might imagine. They can stun sizeable prey with it—render undersea creatures unconscious and easy to eat. The dolphin is not itself an undersea creature, but an air-breather; unconsciousness means death (unless the victim is buoyed by rescuers and revives quickly). Any dolphin from adolescence on has the constant and instant power to kill any other nearby dolphin. In thousands of years of keen human observation, no such act has ever been recorded or suggested.

This is social responsibility. And in a creature whose information is so free it is essentially free from misuse. The dolphin shows us the virtue of openness and trust, the rightness of the difficult path of personal freedom.

Issues as big as lies and freedom are teleological. Certainly no one cares to claim we're only a few hundred years from solving the problems of license and fascism, libertarianism and self-defense. So take the long view: the dolphins solved them! (They have only man to fear now, they've conquered themselves.) What reason is there to believe that humans would fail, if they went a similar way, over the aeons?

To knit this fore-word up with the main-words to come, from Swan and Peattie, it is necessary only to point out: the social responsibility (the restraint, the selflessness) of the dolphin evolved along with and to as high a degree as their "know everything and say anything" freedom of information. Their social responsibility is complete and their information is as free as the word can mean on this earth. As dolphins evolved, understanding each other more, they loved and forgave more. So you be not afraid to let go.

And the large-brained bipeds such as those who debated in New Orleans? Of social responsibility and freedom of speech, it's not which wins but that both do. When the proponents of no limits to the interpretation of one's own experience permit the emergence of harmful ideas that others then exploit, socially responsible individuals act. They are morally not inferior to the—shall we tag them—libertarians. They are eternal counterparts.

And as with the dolphin, human social responsibility and freedom of information—knowledge and forgiveness—develop together, invigorating each other. The world that humans evolve toward—teleologically speaking, of course, only the midterm future—may find them brained with the ability to assay the impact of a thing in the same moment they conceive of it. Action and reaction considered simultaneously: this is very little to ask of brains our size.

So there can be no winner in this debate. There must be none. What there must be is never-ending contention, no doubt bitter and desperate at times, and perpetually exhausting—what better expense of the renewable resource that is life than the contentions of growth?—but never victorious. A people, a life-form, an Order upon the Void will perish without accident, surprise, rough-rubbing. Exclusion, refusal—these are markers of death. So the no limits people must be unbowed. Yet why destroy vast accomplishments—civilization, for example—by letting wild plans be enacted out of "fairness". . . ? So the "responsible" ones must be trusted and encouraged. If either should "win," life is doomed.

To conclude this cetological excursion, the forewordist

fantasizes that his own view has been solicited. He does not believe his tendencies are not discernible throughout the foregoing prose, but does imagine that the reasons for them could be of interest. They are, that:

The prow of the New, the Chance, dulls as it is propelled through the flame of time. In the far reaches, time will have stopped it: corroded the point, flattened it, worn the prow finally to a plow, brought the New to unmoving cold. This "time," this friction, has other names: heat death, obligation, responsibility, connotation. From all life, or order, must come death someday. The "socially responsible," letting misadventures persuade against adventures, *will* win some far away day, herding us back to the formless void, plowing bright chance to a halt. I see the libertarian's cause as a sacred, a martyred one: postponement — and for what purpose can it be but love, or joy? — of the inevitable chill. Prolongation of life, that wisp of frail brave lichen on the rock of world.

Bekämen doch die Lügner alle
Ein solches Schloss vor ihren Mund:
Statt Hass, Verleumdung, schwarzer Galle,
Bestünde Lieb' und Brüderbund.

If all liars had such a
lock on their mouths,
instead of hate, slander, black bile,
there would be love and brotherhood.

— Mozart, "Die Zauberflöte" (via Noel Peattie)

In short, Sir, I have got no further than this:
Every man has a right to utter what he thinks truth,
and every other man has a right to knock him
down for it. Martyrdom is the test.

— Samuel Johnson, in Boswell's *Life* (via John Swan)

Untruth or Consequences

*John Swan**

A few years ago an Illinois man named Paul Heinrich became so angry with a certain young woman of his acquaintance that he took the unusual step of producing and distributing a leaflet about her. In that document he called her a promiscuous, drug-using social deviate and an unfit mother who ought to have her daughter taken away from her. He also wrote a letter to the woman's mother, calling her "mother of a whore," "grandmother of a bastard," and "white trash." Just to make things perfectly clear, he added, "I hope to God you take me to court for distributing the enclosed newsletter."[1]

Heinrich's prayer was answered. He was charged in McLean County for criminal defamation under the Illinois Criminal Code. At this point the case began to get interesting to lawyers and, incidentally, librarians. According to the statute in question (Ill. Rev. Stat. 1981, Ch. 38, par. 27-1), a criminal libel defendant must not only show that his offending utterance is true, but also that he did the deed with "good motivation" and for "justifiable ends." This "qualified truth defense," as lawyers call it, is mandated not only by the law but also by the Illinois Constitution.

Heinrich moved that the charges against him be dismissed on the grounds that this chink in the armor of a defense based upon the truth was a violation of the First and Fourteenth Amendments to the U.S. Constitution. The circuit court agreed and dismissed the

*Reprinted from Library Journal, *July 1986; copyright © 1986 by Reed Publishing, USA, Div. of Reed Holdings, Inc. This is an edited version of a paper delivered at the 1985 conference on "The Politics of Information" at Indiana University, Bloomington.*

1

charges. On appeal, the Illinois Supreme Court reversed the decision and upheld the statute.

The U.S. Supreme Court refused to take *The People of the State of Illinois* v. *Paul Heinrich* under review. This probably means that Paul Heinrich will be taken to trial back in McLean County and whatever the outcome there, this landmark libel case will make its way back to the Supreme Court via another appeal.

A lot of people are interested in the outcome, particularly those who have a healthy dislike of a law that imposes "criminal liability on a declarant, regardless of the truthfulness of the statements made or the declarant's knowledge of the truth or falsity of those statements."[2] The Freedom to Read Foundation has agreed with the assertion of the defense that this is bad business. Truth *must* be an absolute defense in such cases for a number of vital First Amendment reasons. Otherwise libel action could stop the flow of necessary information merely on the grounds that those releasing it have difficulty proving they are properly motivated to tell the truth.

The Freedom to Read Foundation has put money into this case, money that is largely from, and for the sake of, us librarians. We should applaud this investment. Truth is the most precious commodity in the information market for practical as well as idealistic reasons — the "truth" here being that of Mill, Milton, and Socrates, not the far more common version, which Ambrose Bierce defined as "an ingenious compound of desirability and appearance."[3]

The commitment of librarians to the truth as an absolute legal defense should never be confused with our basic professional commitment to the flow of all kinds of information without regard to its truth or falsehood. One of the Freedom to Read Foundation lawyers made that important observation when the Foundation affirmed its support for the defense in *Heinrich*.

Truth may be, must be, an absolute criterion under the law, but it has no such place in the selection, classification, storage, and weeding decisions made by librarians.

One hopes it is self-evident that we are not arbiters of the truth. The first tenet of the Library Bill of Rights, our primary professional interpretation of the Constitution as it applies to us (and our patrons), states that:

> Books and other library resources should be provided for the interest, information, and enlightenment of all people of the community the library serves. Materials should not be excluded because

of the origin, background, or views of those contributing to their creation.

The document's second point commits us to a broad diversity and tolerance:

> Libraries should provide materials and information presenting all points of view on current and historical issues. Materials should not be proscribed or removed because of partisan or doctrinal disapproval.[4]

These statements make no reference to the truth or untruth of library materials, and that is as it must be. Another ALA document, "Diversity in Collection Development," a particularly vital and hard-won interpretation of the Library Bill of Rights, addresses this point most directly:

> Intellectual freedom, the essence of equitable library services, promotes no causes, furthers no movements, and favors no viewpoints. It only provides for free access to all expressions of ideas through which any and all sides of a question, cause, or movement, may be explored. Toleration is meaningless without tolerance for what some may consider detestable.[5]

This openness is necessary simply because Ambrose Bierce was right: the real world offers us a multiplicity of "truths" compounded of desirability and appearance, often contradictory, sometimes in violent conflict with one another. As human beings we inevitably hold cause with one or many of these truths, but as librarians our cause is, in a very practical sense, not truth but freedom. Indeed, our truth *is* freedom, freedom of access, freedom for our patrons to draw upon our resources, to sort their own truths out of our carefully collected and managed mélange of truths, half-truths, untruths, and nontruths.

It takes very little knowledge of the development of the library profession to realize that this position is the result of slow evolution and hard politics.

The renowned and influential librarian of the San Francisco Free Public Library, F.B. Perkins, was expressing the dominant sentiment of the profession when he wrote, "I say that a Free Public Library has no business to furnish licentious, immoral, or vulgar

books.... A Free Public Library is an education institution.... Its
first requisite is, therefore, that it should be useful — should do good;
its office as to amusement is of very minor importance. The business
of teaching immorality it ought not to practice at all."[6] Perkins
asserted this belief in a particular set of library truths almost exactly
one hundred years ago.

If the library profession's current official policy statements are
to be believed, we have evolved as a profession from the position of
guardians of one set of truths to guardians of access to all information.[7]

It is paradoxical, then, if also somewhat platitudinous, that the
librarian's duty is as much to preserve the untruth on the shelves as
the truth. But it cannot be denied that Perkins's delineation of the
moral chasm between "Free Libraries and Unclean Books" has a
contemporary ring to it, despite its century of age.

Perkins is certainly echoed by many today who devote themselves to translating their religious and social convictions into pressure for the censorship of other people's religious and social convictions. This external pressure, however, is only part of the problem.
The process of accommodating mutually exclusive versions of the
truth can be a most challenging exercise in political communication.

The sharper issue here, however, is not the external push and
pull, but the complications that arise from our personal allegiances.
We do indeed bring our own versions of the truth to the job. We
don't put them behind us when we make professional judgments.
Selection and weeding and organizing and providing access and
guidance are all carried out with at least one eye cocked on the truth,
or at least a consensus thereof established by the review media,
public opinion, and other measures.

We prefer to buy books that tell the truth about life or dog
grooming or history or solar panels, rather than those which distort,
mislead, lie, or just make mistakes.

Demand is obviously important also, but demand is itself
usually conditioned by some ingredient of truth, whether it is that
perceived by a few scholars or that mirrored in the desires and
dreams of a multimillion Harlequin readers.

This truth is older than Plato: People do not deliberately seek
falsehood, however twisted a thing they make of the truth they do
seek. In itself, this is not the problem, but it leads to the problem,
which is a deep, even structural ambiguity in our commitment to

untruth as it is presumably protected by those first two tenets of the Library Bill of Rights.

There is much more to this issue than the old and unresolvable clash between ideal standards and real practices. It is a problem with concrete professional and political implications. They can be demonstrated by way of a recent and usefully notorious case in California — especially useful because it involves a group with a mission that is just about as free of the truth as any defender of untruth could wish for.

In June 1984, David McCalden, the guiding spirit of an organization called Truth Missions, contracted with the California Library Association to rent exhibit space and to reserve a meeting room at the December CLA convention.

In September, after considerable discussion and pressure from Jewish and other sympathetic, outraged groups, the California Library Association cancelled McCalden's contract. In October he responded with a threat to sue them for breach of contract and again, on advice from counsel, the CLA Conference Planning Committee voted to rescind the cancellation. This in turn resulted in widespread protest, threats from extremist groups, and a banner headline in the *Los Angeles Times*. A resolution passed by the Los Angeles City Council stated that:

> While we must protect the right of all Americans to express their views, there is no obligation to provide the forces of hatred such respected platforms. We therefore call on the California Library Association to recognize their grave error of judgment and urge them to remove these individuals from their program.[8]

The City Council backed this suggestion with a threat to withdraw all support, "formal or informal," from CLA.

As you could guess, the California Library Association decided again, finally, to cancel the Truth Missions contract. In the letter of cancellation CLA Executive Director Stefan Moses used an escape clause in the contract allowing CLA "to restrict exhibits that may be objectionable or to order the removal of any portion of an exhibit which in the judgment of the association is detrimental to or detracts from the general order of exhibits."[9] The hollow ring to this statement is the sound of librarians caving in.

The California Library Association had itself sent McCalden the regular exhibitor's packet at the suggestion of one of its members because he had been denied space to exhibit his banned books during the 1983 observation of Banned Books Week by the Torrance Public Library. The CLA knew what he had to offer, and it was not McCalden who was detracting from the "order of exhibits" but the host of protesters aroused by what he had to offer.

Just what did McCalden have to offer? Truth Missions is dedicated to the proposition that the Holocaust is an entirely over-rated event, and that evidence for it is largely a fabrication of a vast Zionist conspiracy. (McCalden refers to the American Jewish Com-mittee as the "Kosher nostra.")

Formerly a leader of the notorious Institute for Historical Review, which through such books as *The Hoax of the Twentieth Century* has reviewed the Holocaust right out of history, McCalden does admit that some Jews died in concentration camps, mostly of starvation and disease when times were tough for everybody near the end of the war. He claims, however, that no Jews were gassed to death in the concentration camps, that the gas was used only to delouse clothing.

It was McCalden who, in 1979, issued the challenge of a $50,000 prize to anyone providing proof that any Jews were put to death in the gas chambers at Auschwitz. McCalden used the name Lewis Brandon at that time. A Los Angeles businessman and Auschwitz survivor, Mel Mermelstein, took up the challenge and provided the proof—rejected, of course, by McCalden but accepted by a Los Angeles Superior Court in an important suit.[10] (The case is still in the courts on appeal.)

The banning of the Truth Missions banned-books display and meeting has a disproportionate place in my argument precisely because of the utter lack of truth to the message peddled by McCalden and his ilk. The point here is not to chastise the Califor-nia Library Association. Their waffling had the virtue of self-examination, and it is doubtful whether any similar organization would have behaved differently under the circumstances.

True, one thinks immediately of the American Civil Liberties Union and its brave and almost ruinous tenacity in attacking what was essentially an unconstitutional parade ordinance used against the Nazis in Skokie. But part of the point here is that the ACLU and a library association are not similar organizations.

In a letter to the *Los Angeles Times,* Ramona Ripston, execu-tive director of the Southern California American Civil Liberties Union, asserted that the California Library Association, as "a private group, does not have to permit David McCalden to speak at its conference." She went on to add: "However, the ACLU remains committed to the principle that freedom of thought also includes freedom for those ideas we hate."

This sounds like our very own *Intellectual Freedom Manual.* Ripston cites Woodrow Wilson in words that reflect the healthy reasoning behind her position:

> I have always been among those who believe that the greatest freedom of speech was the greatest safety, because if a man is a fool, the best thing to do is to encourage him to advertise the fact by speaking.[11]

Jeff Selth, librarian at the University of California, Riverside, and chair of the Southern California Coalition for Intellectual Freedom, in a long, arduous letter to the *Los Angeles Times* defending McCalden's right to a place at the convention, maintained that

> my beliefs about the Holocaust were totally irrelevant, since all I was doing was defending free speech, as I will do for everybody, regardless of their views, since that is supposed to be the American way.[12]

Those are brave words — especially considering that the chancellor of Selth's place of employment had a letter in the same *Times* issue. Like most everyone else, the chancellor managed to divorce the Nazis from free speech, noting that he was "gratified" that the California Library Association recognized the "distinction between freedom of speech, which no one disputes, and the obligation to provide a forum for a person whose views have been repudiated as neo-Nazi propaganda by recognized academic authorities."[13]

The ACLU is devoted to the preservation of civil liberties; that is an extremely difficult legal, political, and social commitment. Librarians are devoted to putting those civil liberties into practice, and that is a different sort of commitment. Once the ACLU had seen where its path lay in the Skokie case, it took only relentless legal warfare and appalling courage to stick to it.

Librarians, on the other hand, must confront political and social reality in a very different way. Remember the marvelous dictum of Mark Twain: "It is by the goodness of God that in our country we have those three unspeakably precious things: freedom of speech, freedom of conscience, and the prudence never to practice either of them."[14] It will not do to underrate prudence, even this embarrassing kind, because we all rely on it heavily. They certainly did in California.

So what is the California problem doing in the middle of an argument about the importance of untruth to librarians? After all, external pressure had more to do with CLA's welching on McCalden than any internal distaste for his mission. While the real issue is related both to the external protest and to internal intolerance, it is distinct from both.

We are caught in a dilemma that we have generally failed to appreciate: We are committed both to the search for the truth and to the freedom of expression of untruth. It is a truism that these commitments are not mutually contradictory, that they are, in fact, necessary to one another. However, when they are translated into real political terms, they often, in fact, collide. Like the Los Angeles City Council and that Riverside chancellor, many people are ready to grant the untruth some theoretical place in the network of free debate, but no place that will somehow grant that untruth legitimacy.

In the political arena, belief in the corrective powers of the marketplace of ideas is rapidly supplanted by a fear that bad ideas, especially bad ideas that excite base instincts, will drive out good ideas. This is not merely an irrational fear. A quick glance at the world of politics could lead to the conclusion that the bad ideas have taken the field.

Bad ideas certainly had a field day in Nazi Germany. But Hitler did not rise to power as the result of a contest of ideas. Is it not obvious that grim forces well beyond the reach of ideas were at work to select out and promote the worst elements in that society? Is it not also obvious that the worst ideas prevailed, not because they were aired, but because they had the forces of coercion and fear behind them. As the brutal stifling of debate progressed, the hold of untruth became stronger.

This connection was made more eloquently by another interested party in the McCalden debate. Elli Wohlgelernter, editor of the *B'nai B'rith Messenger,* in splendid, lonely sentiments, put it this way:

> Was something really accomplished by denying him his lunatic pronouncements? And is our community really better off because we

shut him up? . . . Having already invited him, a library should never "cave in" based on the unpopularity of an idea. Or do we agree with those who would ban Mark Twain from libraries? Where do we draw the line? Let the marketplace of ideas determine the validity of an argument, not the prior censorship of its presentation. What next? Do we burn the books? Or have we forgotten the lessons of 50 years ago, that where they would burn books, they would soon burn people.[15]

Our task is to convince ourselves and our public that this must be the basis of our practical library politics as well as good theory. It is essential to this process of conviction that we truly grant a place in the intellectual freedom scheme of things for that which we *know* to be untrue.

The simple theoretical point is, as the *Intellectual Freedom Manual* tells us, that freedom is indivisible. Yet even as we assert this, we know in our collections, our meetings, and our hearts, that we must live with a more or less distinct hierarchy of truths and untruths. We give more space to the truth. We also tend to evaluate each item, each idea, each datum according to that hierarchy.

I *know* that there is no truth to Truth Missions, but if that alone is the determining factor for my treatment of their ideas, my treatment is not likely to conform to that necessary indivisibility of freedom. There are a lot of influential people who *know* that abortion is murder, and some of them liken abortion-on-demand to the Holocaust. They are about as interested in maintaining an open forum on the subject as most of us are interested in seriously debating the Nazis.

There is another influential group that *knows* that the theory of evolution is the false doctrine of a powerful cabal of atheist humanists. They have managed to have it demoted and even removed from a number of widely used biology textbooks, which is an indication of their approach to debate—but then, like Phyllis Schlafly's Stop Textbook Censorship Committee, they believe they have been shut out of the marketplace of ideas.

We all have our firm beliefs and commitments. We all *know* some things are true and some are false. This line of reasoning is usually used to support the practical relativism that we all adopt to some degree in a world where we generally have no choice but to see through a glass darkly. That which looks false today may tomorrow be found to be true. History is full of that sort of thing. Ask any member of the Flat Earth Society. This argument is not good enough. We are not defending the presence of untruth in our libraries just because it might turn out to be true.

McCalden's arguments will never turn out to be true, and "Creation science" will always be apologetics masquerading as empiricism, but both have a place in our libraries.

The crisis in the California Library Association reminded many of the storm that surrounded the American Library Association film, *The Speaker*. One of the problems with that troubled ALA intellectual freedom film is that it puts a great deal of emphasis on the argument that today's falsehoods may be tomorrow's truths. Mildred Dunnock wisely intones to her beleaguered student lecture committee that some of our greatest truths were first rejected as foolishness, and that is why it is so important that this man be allowed to speak.

The man is a racist modeled upon a real-life, much-censored proponent of racial hierarchies. The brave little teacher is right, of course, to defend his right to speak, but her argument is one dimensional, as oversimplified as the political situation the film portrays. The speaker has a right to speak, not because his brand of racism just may be one of those truths waiting for vindication, but he also has the right to utter untruths that will never be vindicated. The suppression of any idea can be dangerous to the flow of all ideas.

This is not merely purist pontification; it is the necessary consequence of the fact that we do see through a glass darkly. Someone has said that the truth may be simple, but *we* are complex, and therefore our paths to the truth must be complex. Our road map is a bewildering maze of smudged and partial truths thoroughly enmeshed in falsehoods. To stumble upon a whole truth is a rare and lucky event, and we're usually not equipped to appreciate it. In this state of affairs bad ideas and untruths are a necessary part of the search. Like mosquitoes — nasty, sometimes fatal malaria mosquitoes, if you will — they may be utterly detestable, but they are a vital ingredient in the overall ecology. To suppress them is to affect the ecology of the whole system of discourse.

This is not to say that many restrictions and compromises are not necessary, just as it has proven necessary to extinguish, or try to extinguish, some of the most malevolent forms of life. But there are always tradeoffs.

The effort to kill off an untruth by suppressing its expression is always risky. For example, child pornography is a very serious problem which anyone with any claim to healthy humanity considers to be an expression of purest untruth. The Supreme Court chose to attack this untruth with a sweeping declaration that it is unprotected speech. The *Ferber* decision was 9 to 0 in favor of broadly defined suppression, but it is doubtful whether this noble unanimity has had any serious effect upon the flow of this particular untruth. It has certainly made its mark on the world of legitimate publishing, as witness the suppression of *Show Me* and other sex education materials.

Note also the growing acceptance in schools of the expurgated *Romeo and Juliet,* the original of which is literally actionable in the terms of the *Ferber* decision. The political potency of this decision is demonstrated in a small but telling way by the fact that we Indiana librarians have been unable to find a legislative sponsor for our affirmative defense amendment to the state's child pornography law, a similarly all-encompassing spawn of *Ferber.*

No one wants to be associated with this evil in any way, even to secure a straightforward, even traditional defense for libraries, museums, and other educational institutions. We are assured that the law is not aimed at "real literature." Apparently those 400 words in *Romeo and Juliet* are a small price to pay for a political kiester.

It is our job to provide access not to the truth, but to the fruit of human thought and communication; not to reality, but to multiple representations thereof. Truth and reality must fend for themselves within each of the complicated creatures who uses the materials we have to offer. We can and do learn a great deal from bad ideas and untruths.

It is obvious enough that we learn about the motivations and the twisted psyches of those who cherish them. Late in his life Ezra Pound admitted something to Allen Ginsberg that is to the point: "The worst mistake I made was that stupid, suburban prejudice of anti–Semitism." Ginsberg replied,

> It's lovely to hear you say that ... because anyone with any sense can see it as a humour, in that sense part of the drama, a model of your consciousness. Anti-Semitism is your fuck-up ... but it's part of the model and the great accomplishment was to make a working model of your mind. Nobody cares if it's Ezra Pound's mind but it's a mind like everybody's mind.[16]

It takes a clarity, an enormous tolerance to learn so much from the struggle with untruth, but we would do well to try it ourselves, even as we know that Ezra Pound's mind is not like everybody's mind, and antisemitism is a disease not like everyone else's diseases.

We shall inevitably and properly give our personal and professional preference to the truth, but it is vital that we recognize the place of untruth in helping us get at the truth. In most of the controversies before us the difficulty of the issue, the heat of the debate, and the pressure from one or all sides to rig the debate by silencing the opposition are all directly proportional.

According to the introductory lines of the Library Bill of Rights, "all libraries are forums for information and ideas." This phrase is the bland fruit of compromise, but it does make the point: We provide an arena for debate; very often we are both the battlefield and the arsenal in the war of ideas; we very naturally and humanly get caught up in the cause of one side or another. We are prochoice or prolife, proevolution or pro-creation, even pro- and anticensorship. Although this is another platitude, it must be said: We are all protruth. That is why we support the truth as an absolute defense in a defamation case involving a very emotional man who took the distasteful step of writing some nasty things about a young woman.

It is this simple fact that we are committed to the truth that makes it utterly necessary that we formulate our mission as librarians not in terms of truth but in terms of access. It is why we must make it clear to ourselves and our public that access means a professional responsibility to, among other things, as much untruth as we can politically and practically manage.

We live within a freedom necessarily circumscribed by many legal and political realities, as the California librarians have helpfully reminded us. It is a real and precious freedom. McCalden is wrong when he says, "there is no free speech in America."[17] But to the extent that there is no free speech for *him,* for all the other hate-mongers, the racists, or those who could coerce us with their version of god, McCalden has a point, and we have a problem.

The knowledge of truth and the knowledge of untruth, like the knowledge of good and evil, are indissolubly joined. Our cause, professionally and politically, is with both of them.

References

1. *The People of the State of Illinois* v. *Paul Heinrich,* Docket No. 59239, Agenda 11, May 1984, p. 2. Quoted in opinion of the court delivered by Justice Moran. Materials provided here by the ALA Office for Intellectual Freedom and the Freedom To Read Foundation.
2. Brief and Argument for Defendant-Appellee, No. 59239 in the Supreme Court of Illinois, p. 2.
3. Bierce, Ambrose, *The Devil's Dictionary.* 1911; reprint, Dover, 1958, p. 136.
4. *Intellectual Freedom Manual.* American Library Association, 1983, p. 14.
5. *Ibid.,* p. 43.
6. Perkins, F.B., *Free Libraries and Unclean Books.* San Francisco Free PL, November 22, 1885, p. 3–4. This copy of the pamphlet located in the *Tuttle Miscellany,* vol. 100, Wabash College.
7. For an excellent account of the evolution of the profession in this regard, see Evelyn Geller, *Forbidden Books in American Public Libraries, 1876–1939.* Greenwood, 1984.
8. Kamm, Susan, "'Holocaust hoax' publisher barred from annual convention of California LA after controversy spreads through state," *American Libraries,* January 1985, p. 5.
9. *Ibid.*
10. Beck, Melinda, "Footnote to the Holocaust," *Newsweek,* October 18, 1981, p. 73.
11. Ripston, Ramona, Letters to the Times, *Los Angeles Times,* November 26, 1984, pt. 2, p. 4. This and several of the following citations courtesy of McCalden himself, who devoted an issue of his *Revisionists' Reprints* (no. 8, January 1985) to off-prints of a large number of the press responses to his "martyrdom"— including many columns very unfavorable to him: he may be "using" the First Amendment, but at least he does so with some consistency. Naturally, this particular issue of his serial was treated to a special mass mailing for fundraising purposes. McCalden has decided to ride the issue further by fulfilling everyone's worst expectations and taking the California Library Association to court; the case is still there and already a considerable drain on the resources of the association.
12. Selth, Jeff, *ibid.*
13. Aldrich, Daniel G., Jr., *ibid.*
14. Twain, Mark, *Following the Equator: A Journey Around the World.* vol. 1, Harper, 1899, p. 198. (Headnote to Chapter XX, ascribed to "Pudd'nhead Wilson's New Calendar.")
15. Wohlgelernter, Elli, "Free Speech," *B'nai B'rith Messenger,* November 23, 1984, p. 14.
16. Quoted in James J. Wilhelm, *Il Miglior Fabbro: The Cult of the Difficult in Daniel, Dante, and Pound.* University of Maine Press, 1982, p. 96. Originally in *Evergreen Review,* vol. 55, 1968, Michael Reck, "A Conversation Between Ezra Pound and Allen Ginsberg."
17. Quoted in "CLA Cancels 'Holocaust Hoax' Publisher," *Newsletter on Intellectual Freedom,* vol. 34, no. 1, January 1985, p. 31.

Lies, Damned Lies, and Democracy
and The Ethics of Freedom

John Swan

Lies, Damned Lies, and Democracy*

In order to save time and sharpen the focus, let us assume the following points—all of which are obvious enough, but ought to be asserted because of a widespread tendency to reduce the issues before us to a clash between tough-minded social activists on the one hand and naive and feckless purists on the other.

First. The marketplace of ideas is itself a profound and enduring idea, but it is also a flawed and distorted mechanism. The classic statement of the idea itself is, of course, Justice Holmes' dissent to the 1919 *Abrams* decision: "the best test of the truth is the power of thought to get itself accepted in the competition of the market." This statement has behind it a faith in the efficacy of truth that has been expressed by virtually all of our most cherished heroes of intellectual freedom, most cogently by Mill some 60 years before *Abrams:* "Complete liberty of contradicting and disproving our opinion, is the very condition which justifies us in assuming its truth. . . ."[1]

But the dynamics of the real marketplace make that necessary condition, "complete liberty," a most doubtful and rare commodity —and even Holmes' testing process itself has been attacked by, among others, the great libertarian Alexander Meiklejohn, who saw

This is a slightly revised version of the paper given in the original debate with Noel Peattie, New Orleans, July 10, 1988.

15

it as an example of that American obsession, "competitive individualism."[2]

Librarians such as Swan (1979 and 1982)[3] and Peattie (1986)[4] have also agreed that the marketplace acts to exclude or at least occlude important parts of the spectrum of ideas and information. As the past eight years have shown so clearly, the free market has a way of being swallowed up by monopoly capitalism, and the only kind of information that seems to matter is insider information.

Second. There are such things as dangerous and pernicious ideas — not merely lies, but damned lies. Those advocating racism and censorship, for example, have often gained ascendancy in times of crisis; in deadly combination with fear and hatred, such ideas have played a large part in the world's evil. The twentieth century has become the age of the freest and swiftest communication of ideas; it has also been an age of terror and genocide. There is some force, in other words, to Noel's watery metaphor as it surfaced in *Sipapu*[5]: some ideas are carnivorous fish which seek to devour all the other fish in the ocean.

Third. Librarians, like everyone else except nihilists, complete cynics and the utterly values-free, will always try to conduct their business guided by some operative notion of the truth, some devotion to accuracy over inaccuracy, honesty over dishonesty, humane and life-affirming values over the reverse.

Fourth. Librarians, like everyone else without exception, will always conduct their business encircled by more or less severe limitations of time, budget, space, opportunity, and or vision. The truth may be, as William Blake asserted, irresistible once it is properly seen, but precious few of us get anything like a decently uncluttered glimpse.

Given these four points, how does one defend the position that as librarians in a putatively democratic society our chief professional commitment must be to promoting access rather than the truth? Is it that we who believe this are a bunch of relativists, for whom there are no truths, just elements of information? Is it that we have a naive faith that truth has destiny on its side, no matter how unfairly slanted the playing field (borrowing a favorite Ronald Reagan metaphor)? Is it true that we reject all advocacy and lie supine before the manipulators, the liars, the power politicians, and the extremists?

No, no, and no.

Quite to the contrary, we believe that the most effective

advocacy of the truth lies precisely in the act of insuring the widest possible access to all the versions thereof—many of which contain no truth at all. To believe this does *not* mean that we regard the truth merely as a matter for debate. In fact, it has nothing to do with our particular notion of the truth, whether we are pragmatists or idealists, mystics, Platonists, Fundamentalist Baptists or agnostic academics. It *does* mean that debate, dialogue, and exploration are all essential to an understanding of the truth, whatever its nature. It does mean that shutting off exposure to false information and pernicious ideas before they enter the stream of debate will in all likelihood neither kill them nor protect the good ideas they seek to devour.

In his recent book *More Speech: Dialogue Rights and Modern Liberty,* Paul Chevigny offers a usefully lucid set of arguments for the broadest access; he is particularly relevant on the subject of the tolerance of pernicious ideas:

> The question is: Must we tolerate advocacy of ideas that we would under no circumstances put into practice?
>
> The very fact that we say a policy of censorship or genocide is inadmissible under any circumstances implies that we imagine what would happen under such a policy; we know what the alternative to the idea we advocate is and the consequence of our own opinion as well as its opposite. The failure to take the alternative and its consequences into account is to fail to understand our own opinion. If the unacceptable opinion is important enough for us to consider suppressing it, furthermore, it is important enough to answer. It will be connected, through fantasy or linguistic meaning or both, to opinions that some people in the society find attractive; it is essential to come to grips with those fantasies and meanings, to try to explain and answer them. Even though we cannot conceive of the opinion as "true" as a matter of policy, it may be a reflection of social or psychological conflicts that cannot be touched except through a response to those fantasies.... [A]bsolute toleration is a categorical statement that all possibilities can be canvassed when decisions are made.[6]

The strength of Chevigny's argument lies in his recognition of the role which the imagination and understanding must play in the process of grasping the truth. The basic flaw in the position of those who would defeat falsehood by denying it a place in our libraries and library programs is that it fails to take into account the simple but profound fact that the truth must be perceived by individuals, not dictated to them. Certainly there are some ideas which we would rather that no one would advocate ever, but denying the right or the opportunity to advocate them does not expunge them from the minds of those who hold them. Indeed, efforts to deal in this manner with such people—for example, revoking the tenure of some academics who argue that the Holocaust didn't happen—have been more effective in creating martyrs than in isolating dangerous strains of thought.

In one such case in Canada, the Alberta Court of Appeals recently (June of 1988) overturned a decision against a former teacher, Jim Keegstra, who had been convicted of spreading lies about the Holocaust—essentially, that there was no such thing. In his response to this action, the Canadian journalist Tom Regan wrote a column reflecting a change of mind. At first he believed that it was wrong to let people like Keegstra be free to tell malicious lies in public, but he came to be convinced that, in fact, it was more dangerous to censor them. He quoted the testimony of a woman who had been a refugee from Nazi Germany, who came to him with a strong argument against enforced silence:

> ...it's because we had censorship then that we have Jim Keegstra today.... I am old enough to remember when they burned books. There was no freedom of speech at all. Perhaps if there was, it might never have happened. If we had been able to talk about what was going on, people might have seen how it was all lies. But they didn't, and when you had millions of people believing that lie, and no way to combat it ... well, you know what happened. ... [C]ensorship actually creates the Jim Keegstras of the world, rather than destroying them.[7]

The worst falsehoods, the damnedest lies, have their origins not in ideas but in pathologies, and suppressing symptoms does not cure the disease. This is no less true when the disease is virulent and pervasive and systemic. In her brilliant analysis of the relationship between power and sexual violence, "Pornography and Silence,"[8] Susan Griffin makes an essential observation about one particular connection between social and individual pathology that is relevant here:

> It is significant . . . that the moment at which Hitler himself said that he decided he had been born to lead a movement which would restore Germany to racial purity and pride was a cultural moment. He had attended the theatre, for he loved Wagnerian opera. And after a certain performance, moved to tears and near ecstacy at the sight of Teutonic warriors in all their glory, he resolved to himself that he would devote his life to regaining this glory. This culture at one and the same time told him who he was and what he must do.

This is not the place to philosophize about the societal origins of evil in the human consciousness, or about the path from evil (or good) ideas to evil (or good) deeds. Suffice it to say that those who would defeat Nazism by censoring Wagner have an entirely too simple notion of that path. However palpable the connections between words and actions, they are not so direct that simply suppressing the former will eliminate the latter.

"But what," I hear you asking, "does all of this sunlight-is-the-best-disinfectant business have to do with the controversy at hand? We are librarians, not dictators. We are not talking about censorship but about allocating scarce resources within a limited sphere of influence. Some ideas and information are more deserving of those resources than others. Nazis and Klansmen may have First Amendment rights, but they don't have the right to our shelf and program space, any more than do pornographers, or for that matter, all those purveyors of extreme political or religious messages who send us their free literature with such relentless and hopeful generosity."

I hear you, and you speak some truth, at least about the practicalities of librarianship. In spite of impressions to the contrary, no one, not the most rampant purist among us, believes that in our professional commitment to access we are forced into passive acceptance of anything, let alone the unasked-for but well-funded products of super-patriotism and hate-mongering that cross the acquisitions desk. In fact, I personally disapprove of what seems to be a common practice of placing the gift copy of *The Spotlight* on the same rack with the legitimate newspapers. Does this make me a would-be censor of this widely distributed and fervently supported organ of free, albeit racist, thought? Yes, although I wouldn't necessarily throw it away, just demote it to a place for free material that doesn't go through the normal acquisitions process, or give it away to interested parties — which is what I do with sundry Korean, South African, Taiwanese and Middle Eastern progaganda, and the

Executive Intelligence Review—despite the $10 price tag printed on the cover—which, thanks to the multidisciplinary nature of Lyndon LaRouche's editorializing, I have sent to friends in music and biology as well as on the political science faculty, mostly on the theory that one's amusement ought to be shared. And I should make it clear that there is a good deal of free material representing distinct points of view that does go quickly from the mail bag into the trash—a practice that is, I am sure, universal, even among the most libertarian of us junk mail junkies.

How does all this habitual suppression jibe with the argument that we librarians are in the business of assuring access to the widest range of ideas, true, false, or waffling? It is, in fact, thoroughly consistent with the aim of maximizing usable access within given practical restraints. While not denying the strain of censorship which runs through all the above actions, I believe that the various decisions to keep, send on, or pitch are all based more firmly on a set of considerations which are essentially positive in nature. They include research into and judgment about the quality of the material under scrutiny with an eye to the accuracy, the competence, the honesty—indeed, the truth—as reflected therein. They include judgments as to the interests and needs of the audience the library serves (but I believe anyone who limits such judgment to measuring supply and demand and stock turnover ought to consider a career in sales). Then there are the considerations of shelf space, staff time, processing expenditures—and often a fringe magazine gets the current-year-only-don't-bind treatment. But the central issue, more important than any of these, is the simple question, "Is access to the point of view represented in this material useful in some way to the patrons of this library?"

There is seldom a simple answer to this question; often it is unknowable beforehand—and "useful" is a deliberately vague term in any case. The elements of the decision which I have described are undoubtedly familiar, and so is the ambiguity. Indeed, the trouble with this homely litany of small decisions and big compromises is just that it seems no different from any workaday set of library procedures, uninformed by any higher vision. But its familiarity should not obscure the fact that this process is impelled by a positive intention: the will to preserve the broadest useful access to information and ideas—including, if that access is relevant, to disinformation and bad ideas.

There is a common perception—enunciated by Noel Peattie,

among others—that the "liberal paradox" is a fatal flaw in the reasoning of those of us who would tolerate the full range of ideas, including, that is, those carnivorous fish, ideas that would bring an end to free expression of other ideas. If it is a flaw, it is certainly well recognized in the canons of libertarianism. An example is another famous Holmes dissent, that in *Gitlow,* in which the judge pursues the logic and accepts the conclusion:

> If, in the long run, the beliefs expressed in proletarian dictatorship are destined to be accepted by the dominant forces of the community, the only meaning of free speech is that they should be given their chance and have their way.[9]

Now it is true that Holmes was referring to communism, a fairly horrific prospect to the majority then and now in this country, but not of the category of pure evil occupied by the aforementioned racism and genocide. Holmes' point, however, remains valid, because he is delineating the meaning of free speech. There are limits to free speech when speech is translated into action. Our faith in majority rule is girded with qualifications, and the majority that favors genocide has no right to put the idea into practice—not that rights, or ideas for that matter, play much of a part in this particular practice, anyway.

But the tolerance of intolerant and even intolerable ideas is not a flaw in the libertarian scheme of things. It is a cornerstone of the whole structure of liberty. The endless paradoxes and compromises which arise from it cannot be avoided through the imposition of general exemptions, however finely crafted. To command that certain ideas not be expressed does not purify the atmosphere of free thought; it encloses it and renders it stale. Our endless attempts at legal purification in the realms of obscenity and pornography, for example, have so far brought comfort only to those who have little truck with free thought anyway.

These observations apply with equal force to the world of and the role of the library. We apply all sorts of restrictions in the allocation of our resources, but if we do so according to a policy which claims for us a right to deny access on the grounds of our notion of just which ideas are too dangerous to tolerate, we are working against, not for, intellectual freedom. We are betraying not only the commitment to free access, but also the unfettered search for the truth itself, whatever its nature.

One of the deepest problems with the library profession's sense of itself is, I believe, its failure to come to terms with what it means to make decisions as a professional. For myself, I define that decision-making process by borrowing a favorite view of intelligence: "Intelligence is measured not by what you know but what you do when you don't know." We librarians know a lot, as we must, but we tend to distrust and to avoid the large questions and dilemmas that hover not very far over our heads and concentrate exclusively in the endless details, clerical, technical, technological, managerial, of our work, as if we will solve all the problems worth solving by rooting out clear answers and procedures. The ruling models, perhaps, are the vast and detailed LC schedules, the place-for-everything-and-everything-in-its-place world of Dewey Decimal (although any cataloguer can tell you that in this endeavor, too, applying the scheme to the reality is fraught with choice and ambiguity). The fact is that there are vital issues which we must confront, often in pressing circumstances, which do not yield themselves to clear procedures; despite the illumination shed upon them by our abundant and hard-won professional training, the final decision must be a leap into what we do not know.

There are those who believe that they can devise noble universal principles of advocacy that exclude damned lies, or deny communication of ideas with pernicious regimes, and thereby concentrate their resources upon those worthier of free expression. The idea is tempting, not unlike the idea that you ought to be able to slip a warning label into a racist or sexist book according to some general principle of right thinking. But it is nothing more, I believe, than another manifestation of this distrust of the real act of independent decision-making. Our shared belief in freedom of expression ought somehow to produce simple and clear decisions, and sometimes it does, although simple and clear can also mean tough and courageous. But often in the daily round of librarianship, the belief in intellectual freedom means clinging tenaciously to a principle while pursuing it through indirection and compromise. That principle is not, cannot be, "Let me provide the truth." It must be, "Let me provide access."

It is ironic that we librarians debate the place of dangerous and extreme ideas in our corner of the world of communication, when we are so sorely needed as champions of access. This is a time in which the Meese Pornography Commission recommendations are being turned into repressive laws, government secrecy is burgeoning while public access to information is dwindling, and media monopolies threaten diversity while their television and newspaper components continue to narrow the spectrum of what is deemed "newsworthy." In our underfunded and overcompromised way, we provide one of the best hopes for democratic access, and incidentally, one of the best chances for each among those who use us to find an individual version of the truth. In our devotion to the broadest scope of access we are taking risks, but we are not helpless before the liars, the bigots and the manipulators. We simply refuse to adopt their tactics; we refuse to respond to their intolerance with ours. That is our strength, our truth.

References

1. Mill, John Stuart, *On Liberty* (1859), in *Three Essays* (Oxford: Oxford University Press, 1975), p. 27.
2. Meiklejohn, Alexander, *Political Freedom* (Oxford University Press, 1965), as quoted by Paul Chevigny in *More Speech: Dialogue Rights and Modern Liberty* (Philadelphia: Temple University Press, 1988), p. 7.
3. Swan, John C., "Librarianship Is Censorship," *Library Journal*, vol. 104, no. 14, October 1, 1979, pp. 2040–43; and "Ethics at the Reference Desk: Comfortable Theories and Tricky Practices," *Ethics and Reference Services*, ed. Bill Katz and Ruth Fraley (New York: Haworth Press, 1982; also published as *Reference Librarian*, no. 4), pp. 99–116.
4. Peattie, Noel, "Cardinal Mazarin Is Dead?!" *Sipapu*, vol. 17, no. 2 (1986), pp. 11–17. Of course, the whole existence and noble tenure of *Sipapu* is testimony to the narrowness of the mainstream, since its purpose is to increase awareness of the "alternative" press.
5. Peattie, p. 17.
6. Chevigny, pp. 121–122.
7. Regan, Tom, "Censorship Can Create Keegstras," *The Daily News* (Halifax), Tuesday, June 21, 1988.
8. Griffin, Susan, *Made from This Earth: An Anthology of Writings by Susan Griffin* (New York: Harper and Row, 1982), p. 156.
9. Quoted in Haiman, Franklyn S., *Speech and Law in a Free Society* (Chicago: University of Chicago Press, 1981), p. 272.

The Ethics of Freedom; or,
The Practicalities of Free Access*

As has already been demonstrated, it doesn't take a radical's vision to recognize that there are often collisions between freedom and the free market—and that includes the idea market. What deserves further exploration is the strategy by which we seek to in-sure freedom even for ideas with little or no power in the market. The strategy is largely unconscious, but nonetheless a strategy, a more-or-less consistent method of sorting ideas and information and promoting access to some of them while inevitably hindering or at least neglecting others. In other words, we play a far from "neutral" role in the information flow, even if our commitment to ideological neutrality in providing access has the personal status of an abiding ethical standard.

Although we have pointed to the obvious and important every-day practicalities of this process of balancing usefulness, access, and freedom, it may be valuable to restate the approach in terms of the ethical fabric of which it is a part. Let us begin with politics:

> "Don't join the book-burners.
> Don't think you are going to conceal thoughts
> by concealing evidence that they ever existed."
> (Dartmouth College, June 14, 1953)

President Dwight Eisenhower's stirring call to courage, uttered during the dark times of McCarthy's infection paranoia, has long been a reassuring presence in the literature of intellectual freedom. For instance, it has a place of honor in the 1988 Banned Books Week publicity book as one of many immortal quotations to draw upon in spreading the good word against the current (very healthy) crop of book burners. But Eisenhower directed himself to this subject at Dartmouth only after a long, albeit uneasy, silence. In response to the speech, Senator Herbert Lehman of New York, who for years had been one of the lonely few speaking out against McCarthyism, expressed gladness that the President had "at long last" taken on the censors. He wished him "godspeed . . . if he has chartered a new

The first version of this essay was presented at a seminar sponsored by the Graduate School of Library and Information Studies, Northern Illinois University, September 1988.

course of opposition to these threats to our national life." As Lehman noted, words must be backed with action, however, and in a news conference after the Dartmouth speech, Eisenhower was asked if by "book-burners" he meant Senator McCarthy and his followers. He answered that he never dealt in personalities.

At that time, Senator McCarthy had recently named libraries as a specific target of his brand of patriotism, charging that 30,000 volumes of communist or "fellow-traveling" authors were to be found in State Department-run libraries in foreign countries, part of our overseas information program. He demanded that they be removed. When asked about this at the same post-Dartmouth news conference, Eisenhower replied that he sanctioned the burning of any books in United States government libraries abroad that try to make converts to communism. On this subject, Senator Lehman said, "We have seen the State Department's information centers abroad engage in shameful book-burnings, frantically removing from their shelves books whose authors do not happen to meet the criteria laid down by the little man from Wisconsin and his fellow-travelers."[2]

The point of all this is not to expose unethical behavior — was it, precisely speaking, unethical? — on the part of a still-beloved President, but to draw a parallel. Politicians are, like librarians, creatures of their patrons as well as their consciences. It may be true that public duty and private conscience should coincide, but in fact there are sufficient complexities in both roles to make for constant dilemmas of judgment and of ethics. The two are not synonymous, of course, even in the realm of morality. In his introduction to Robert Hauptman's recent and useful *Ethical Challenges in Librarianship,* Bill Katz puts the matter succinctly: "Ethics is a matter of the good guys and the bad guys." And "given that everyone wants to be counted as a good guy, where is the problem?" The problem, as Katz puts it, is "first and foremost . . . a matter of recognition."[3]

As my brief summary of the contradiction in Eisenhower's words indicates, the recognition issue contains ambiguities on the simplest level. Without daring to probe the real political complexity of the not-so-quiet fifties, I'll accept the view that the nation's leader was, in fact, guilty of a failure of leadership in the McCarthy era. Herbert Lehman certainly thought so, and there is certainly no doubt that the resulting censorship in our libraries here and abroad was a violation of the basic values of our democracy. But was it a failure of character, an ethical matter of fear and avoidance, or was it misjudgment, based on a genuine conviction that the President should be above personalities, and that communism ought to be fought with censorship? It was one of those times, after all, when bad ideas, lies, were in the ascendant, when the majority, or at least the most vocal, in this fragile democracy were thinking and acting in an undemocratic manner, and there is little reason to believe that Eisenhower did not believe with the majority.

The answer is no doubt a mixture of failures in both ethics and politics, but despite the vagueness of this response, the question itself is not trivial. In order to understand an ethical dilemma, it is necessary first to recognize that the problem is an ethical one in the first place. Eisenhower's problem, whether he recognized it or not, did involve the question of ethical decision-making in an area peculiar to democracy. That is, a society which commits itself to freedom of expression for all of its members constantly presents its leaders with choices that affect the freedom of some or all of those members. As John Stuart Mill reminded us, freedom for the majority is not freedom if it is had at the expense of freedom for the minority; therefore, genuine democracy demands that its decision-makers be ever aware that they are engaged in a balancing process, not only between various political forces, but among external strategies and internal standards.

Perhaps these demands are sharper for the public political figure who is called upon explicitly to provide moral leadership, but librarians, too, despite our recessive image, must exert an important kind of leadership, at least within a democracy. Recognizing an ethical dilemma as such, let alone dealing with it, is already a problem for us. As Hauptman and others have noted, ethics has not been a major topic for discussion among librarians: "The literature prior to the mid-seventies is replete with discussions of manners, etiquette, and decorum, but there is little available on specific ethical issues."[4] There is, of course, an official American Library Association Committee on Professional Ethics and an official ALA Code of Ethics, but despite the good works of the former and the forthright, sweeping clarity of the latter, we are a long way from a general understanding of the particular shapes assumed by a library ethics of freedom. The problem is more than one of grasping the general principles of conscientious service, advocacy of the access and privacy rights of patrons, and avoidance of conflict of interest that are writ large in the Code of Ethics. A good illustration of this is to be found in one frank response to the recent censorship survey conducted by the Arkansas Library Association Intellectual Freedom Committee:

> I am employed in a small, rural school where parents are very restricted in thinking about what their children should be learning/reading. Our policy reads that books will support the beliefs, etc. of the community. It kinda cages me in.... My principal feels he has to protect the parents' belief. I feel a greater need to provide varied information to the children. Yet the principal and I both answer to the parents for our jobs and paychecks. It is an incredibly frustrating position. You want to stick your neck out, you know what is right, but it sure is hard to do when actually presented with the opportunity—knowing there is no community support out there.[5]

The author of these lines clearly has a lively appreciation of ethical standards promulgated by the profession, as well as of the practical application of the particular imperative of intellectual freedom enunciated in the *Library Bill of Rights* as well as the Code of Ethics. But there is definitely a problem—and it is not merely that familiar fear of extending the neck. (Indeed, such frank self-examination is a likely sign of courage.)

Echoing the work of Stephen Toulmin and others, Robert Hauptman notes an important aspect of the problem: "The reason that these ethical dilemmas arise is that there is no obvious and absolute resolution to problems. Two or more equally valid solutions pull the librarian in antithetical directions."[6] Like the politician, the librarian must lead as well as respond, and there are ethical considerations attached to both roles. The librarian who forces Karl Marx upon a patron who asked for Groucho is not likely to succeed in broadening that person's intellectual horizons. On the other hand, the librarian who never ventures any acquisitions beyond the safe best-sellers and unthreatening requests has transformed a dynamic professional role into a passive clerkship.

A recent case reported at the Intellectual Freedom Round Table Roll Call of the States had a high school librarian respond to a local outbreak of rumors of witchcraft and satanism—totally unsubstantiated, not that it matters—by withdrawing all the witchcraft books from her library shelves and locking them up, refusing them to any students except those who could prove that they had a specific class assignment requiring them. She is said to have defended this action as entirely consistent with her own sense of professional ethics, despite the fact that she had also served on her state's Intellectual Freedom Committee. A century, even a half-century before this, she would have had a point: the American Library Association and all the powers of culture were once firmly convinced that the librarian's role was to protect the patron from harmful literature as well as to dispense the good (see Evelyn Geller's 1984 *Forbidden Books in Public Libraries* in my bibliography).

The profession has within this century developed a commitment to intellectual freedom that, according to our leading policy documents, is itself an ethical standard. According to that standard, the librarian who takes it upon herself to protect her students from witchcraft books is being professionally unethical, whatever exalted personal standards she is following. This may be clear enough in this instance — it was certainly clear enough to the students who couldn't get at those books — but it is difficult to trace the consequences of that clarity. If this is a case of the violation of professional ethics, is it therefore like other unethical professional behavior, that of the unethical doctor or lawyer, for instance? The librarian is, after all, violating a basic tenet of the profession.

This, too, is not a trivial question, and it is related to the previous nontrivial question, about the nature of Eisenhower's failure, because it, too, has to do with the recognition of an ethical standard as such.

Despite the fact that intellectual freedom is included within our Code of Ethics, it is a standard with a difference. The commandment that "Librarians must resist all efforts by groups or individuals to censor library materials" (Code, Point II) is necessarily sweeping and unqualified, but it is in practice heavily and routinely qualified by every librarian, particularly when we remember that we all do some share of our own censoring. This is not an accusation but a fact of professional life, even for those of us — and it should a lot of us — who regard intellectual freedom as the basic tenet of our business. And herein lies the problem of recognition.

If a librarian sells encyclopedias on the job, or takes money to run a private company's database searches while on the job, or denies information to Republicans that he gives to Democrats, or refuses to serve blacks, or tells his church pastor which people have been checking out books on homosexuality, in other words, if a librarian violates all the other tenets of the Code of Ethics, the nature of the trespass is relatively clear. Whatever the personal motives or extenuating circumstances, these do reduce themselves to a case of the good guys and the bad guys, at least in terms of the acts themselves. Such is also the case with many instances of censorship, self- or otherwise, as with the librarian who locks up the witchcraft books, even if she is adhering to a standard which the profession once held but has in its evolution since shed. All of these acts of commission and omission can be judged by relatively clear standards of fairness, of equity, and found wanting. (This is an oversimplification, but true enough for the purposes of this argument.)

However, beyond the instances of blatant suppression of ideas and information, violations of the ethical commitment to intellectual freedom do not yield themselves so easily to this kind of judgment. Freedom of access itself is not only a distinct standard, such as that of honesty or fairness, but a commitment to a complex of strategies in which one of the ruling considerations is — dare we say it? — that the ends must justify the means. True, there are situations in which we must be dishonest or unfair in the service of a higher ethical goal, but they are exceptions, perhaps not all that rare, even in librarianship, but perceived as exceptions, nonetheless. However, in order to preserve the maximum usable freedom of access, it is necessary to build violations of the literal standard into the very fabric of the practical commitment.

Obvious examples of this occur in the area of acquisitions. Without covering old ground again (covered in my "Librarianship Is Censorship," *Library Journal,* October 1, 1979), I'll restate the unmistakable but somehow controversial point that cultural and ideological screening is an intrinsic part of the process. The librarian who faithfully follows the first sentence of the first article of the *Library Bill of Rights* ("Books and other library resources should be provided for the interest, information, and enlightenment of all people of the community the library serves") will inevitably violate the second sentence of the same article ("Materials should not be excluded because of the origin, background, or views of those contributing to their creation"). This is the situation confronted by the Arkansas school librarian quoted above, and it is not a criticism of the *Library Bill of Rights* itself. The selection process favors the interests of the population for which the selection is done, and it therefore — despite conscientious efforts to expand the horizons of that population — also mirrors to some degree the prejudices and limitations of that community.

If you can show me good, middle American public libraries that represent Marxist Leninism and Islamic culture as fully and fairly on their shelves and in their programs as they do American business capitalism and Christianity, I'll be glad to modify this statement. But if they do manage such laudable diversity and balance, it is very unlikely that their collections in the areas which actually interest their clients are as strong as they ought to be—unless, of course, they are blessed with unlimited acquisitions funds. Again, the point is simple enough, but its significance for the ethical application of the principle of intellectual freedom is seldom appreciated. We inevitably spend our budgets according to priorities that require compromise.

Then there is all that literature we get without spending money. Much of the free material that flows into our libraries is, in fact, useful. Some of it doesn't carry any particular ideological baggage, and therefore the decision whether or not to keep, say, *The Asphalt News* (which I used to send over to a friend in the Drama Department, just to confuse him) will depend upon the potential interest in road surfaces among your patrons, and a negative decision will not imply censorship as such (it is important to keep in mind that weeding and rejecting materials are not intrinsically acts of censorship).

But there is a multitude of governments, political parties, religious groups, poets, novelists, messengers from outer space, and extremists of every stripe who have concluded that their messages are simply too important to trust to our clumsy acquisitions processes. With hearts full of hope, and apparently with pockets full of money, they send us books, journals, flyers, even videotapes, often accompanied by messages that strongly imply that their generosity obligates us to keep and care for their gifts.

There are libraries which keep all of the propaganda they receive, at least within certain categories, to fulfill their missions as scholarly resources. There are also librarians who treat all junk mail as junk, and reject anything that was not specifically ordered for their collections. Within these extremes lies most of the rest of us, who decide what stays and what goes according to considerations of "the interest, information, and enlightenment of all people of the community the library serves," as well as of shelf space and basic manageability. In the process, we screen out most of the extremist material, unless it answers a particular research need; we dump the fringe-group political pamphlets, unless a particular corner of the fringe has a claim on our services; and we try to judge most of the free offerings according to the selection standards that obtain when we are paying. If we failed to do this, if we decided that the librarian's role was to be the passive receptable of all the world's unbidden paper, however unwanted, we would soon be serving our public as badly as if we bought books under the same principle. More to the point, we would be hindering access to ideas and information, not promoting it.

In other words, active rejection according to the ideological and informational content of the materials that cross the acquisitions desk is an inevitable part of maintaining real access to a broad range of ideas. Censorship is a necessary part of management. Indeed, even the person who dooms all the freebies immediately to the dustbin of history cannot avoid the charge. Even if no conscious censorship of individual offerings is involved, a whole category of material is denied consideration on grounds that are, in effect, ideological: the products of the commercial and academic marketplace are given preference over those works which are outside of that relatively normalizing sphere.

With very little effort, this point can be extended to include all of our standard indexes and other access tools, inevitably given preference over the few counter-cultural reference works—a preference further emphasized in the even more commercially conscious world of databases. Many librarians in reference and technical services as well as acquisitions do work to increase awareness of and access to the fringes; they do very important work and there aren't nearly enough of them. But the truth remains that we serve our various populations primarily with what they want and need, and this puts at a considerable disadvantage that which they don't want and don't need, however valuable and important, however deserving of their attention, some of that material is.

Again, it is important to emphasize that selection and collection development which favor one community's world view over all others is not *ipso facto* censorship. There are many positive and negative reasons for choosing and rejecting and weeding that have nothing to do with repressing views. But the fact remains that every librarian shapes the library's collection and its support systems in order to increase the availability of some material at the expense of the readiness of access to other material. A few years ago some members of the extreme right wing in matters political and religious complained to the American Library Association and others that their books and magazines were not available in as many libraries as the works of the left and center. Although a survey of holdings conducted by the Office for Intellectual Freedom demonstrated that most of those conservative titles were available in enough libraries to insure access via interlibrary loan, the protesters still had a point. Access via ILL is simply not the same as immediate access in a library. True, there is a profound difference between delayed gratification and total suppression, but a barrier is still a barrier. If some ideas can't be read about without paperwork and a two-week wait, while others come easily from the shelves, then a form of censorship is in effect.

There is nothing wrong with this, let me quickly add, at least in the world of practical realities and limitations, where it is impossible to provide equal access to all ideas. This is not cause for hand-wringing, but for a heightened awareness of the fact that the process of insuring the maximum access to the ideas and information most likely to be useful and enlightening to a library's community involves the effective suppression and neglect of other ideas and information. This is more than mere market logic; it is an important source of tension that should be part of the critical awareness of every professional. Those who are not aware, who deny the presence of the tension, only conduct their censorship without self-examination. They are not free of it, or of the ethical implications of insuring true intellectual freedom. They who select, and suppress, with a sense of what they are leaving out, and the potential value of that literature to the community they serve, are more likely to compensate, introduce unaccustomed ideas, and bring diversity to the idea pool of the community.

In other words, those who are adequately aware of the dynamism lurking in their theoretically "neutral" ideological role have a better chance at making the library a truly neutral ground for the exploration of ideas and information. There is an irony embedded in the ethics of freedom: In preserving a climate which tolerates the expression of all ideas equally, we are called upon to give space to ideas that are themselves voiced by unethical people or, at best, people who have succumbed to value systems that foster unethical behavior. While we certainly need not tolerate actual unethical behavior in the democratic forum for ideas, we must not create an atmosphere in which the ideas behind that behavior cannot be expressed. This is so even in the face of the above-mentioned practical censorship in which we do engage, and in the face of the fact that our deeper loyalty will always be to the ethical and the true.

We . . . bring our own versions of the truth to the job. We don't put them behind us when we make professional judgments. Selection and weeding and organizing and providing access and guidance are all carried out with at least one eye cocked on the truth, or at least a concensus thereof established by the review media, public opinion, and other measures.[7]

For some, harboring the unethical, granting the lie its place in a forum founded, ideally, for the individual and collective search for the truth, is more than an irony; it is an error, a confusion of an untruth, that which is factually false, with a lie, "a deliberate falsehood uttered to deceive and hurt people."[8] Lies, according to this position, are dangerous to the truth, and to tolerate them in a neutral forum is, in effect, to make "truth a thing to be settled by debate,"[9] and to threaten the whole enterprise of free discourse. It is certainly true that lies can be dangerous, and there is something attractive in the moral thrust of this position (akin to the healthy and forthright intolerance of racist jokes that has made that once highly visible species of witticism a relatively rare thing in social discourse — outside of certain pockets of poverty and high circles of government, that is).

But the old problem remains: Who is to determine which untruths are actually deliberate falsehoods? Who is to decide which statements are lies and which are beliefs, however pathological in origin, for which some are willing to be martyred — and they often convert censorship effectively into martyrdom (as in the case of some of the latter-day Nazis and Holocaust-deniers). Of course, we all agree that the Holocaust was a genuine, if unspeakably terrible, reality, but "we" doesn't include everyone, and if "we" decide by fiat that our truth is never to be assailed by misguided argument, we are not assuring its safety against the outsiders; we are merely converting a perfectly sound truth into an emotional dogma, a distinct step downward in the forum of ideas.

One of my favorite responses in the library censorship survey conducted in Vermont last year (1987) had to do with a concerned parent's objection to a book about communism — to many, a "lie" as venomous as antisemitism — which she found in the town library:

> I talked to the mother, asking her if she preferred her children to
> be enlightened about communism — or to be inveigled into it by not

knowing anything about it. She thought a while, and I heard nothing more. . .

There, in all its simplicity, is the argument for the power of knowledge, of awareness. It is exactly the argument that was lost during the McCarthy madness, overwhelmed by the reverse of the position expressed by this Vermont librarian, the fear that exposure to communism would lead to seduction by it. McCarthy was not entirely wrong about that, of course. Ideas can be dangerous.

But the ethic of freedom is founded on the belief that knowledge is worth the risk. The suppression demanded by McCarthy and abetted, in effect, by the President, was based on a lack of faith in the power of knowledge. This was a bad mistake for politicians. For librarians, for anyone charged with making the full world of knowledge available and possible, it is more than a mistake. It is betrayal of our deepest ethical standard.

References

1. Eisenhower, Dwight D., speech at Dartmouth College, June 14, 1953, as quoted in *Banned Books Week 1988: Celebrating the Freedom to Read,* ed. Robert Doyle (Chicago: American Library Association, 1988), p. 46.
2. Lehman, Senator Herbert, quoted in *The New York Times,* Sunday, June 21, 1953. Story is also source of the information above.
3. Hauptman, Robert, *Ethical Challenges in Librarianship* (Phoenix: Oryx Press, 1988), pp. ix, x.
4. *Ibid.,* p. 1.
5. Kerns, Bettye, and Linda Bly, "Lust in the Dust: Are Our Selections Just?" *Arkansas Libraries,* vol. 44, no. 4, p. 16.
6. Hauptman, p. 2.
7. Swan, John C., "Untruth or Consequences," *Library Journal,* vol. 111, no. 12 (July 1986), p. 47.
8. Peattie, Noel, "Cardinal Mazarin Is Dead?!" *Sipapu,* vol. 17, no. 2 (1986), p. 14.
9. *Ibid.,* p. 16.

Truth, Libraries, and Revolution

Noel Peattie*

I.

Librarians have often encountered writers and speakers who challenge the library profession's claims to the practice of intellectual freedom by insisting that those librarians are actually unfair, that the writers and speakers know the real, hidden truth of a particular issue which librarians are concealing, or that such writers and speakers are an unjustly censored minority. The librarians' professional response, for many decades, has been twofold: a neutral disclaimer, discriminating against no party's viewpoint, and an effort to avoid even the appearance of censorship by the acquisition of materials reflecting a wide spectrum of opinions on controversial subjects.[1]

In recent years the rise of the social responsibilities movement in library work led many to conclude that the traditional neutrality of library professionals not only tended to neglect the voices of ethnic and left-wing dissent, but tended also to weaken the defenses of the profession when faced with authors or speakers whose viewpoints were not simply eccentric, but deliberately fallacious and racist.[2]

A crisis of just this kind arose when David McCalden, a.k.a. Lewis Brandon, an Ulsterman, who had disrupted a British animal protection group, and who had been the only member ever expelled

*A revised and expanded version of the paper given in the original debate with John Swan, New Orleans, July 10, 1988.

from the American Atheists, took up the cause of "Holocaust revisionism": the belief that the destruction of around six million European Jews (plus Romani, gays, communists, and prisoners of war) did not take place on nearly the scale that historians claim that it did. McCalden, and other scholars who make similiar claims, is not simply questioning a statistic: he is describing as illusory one of the major events of the twentieth century. McCalden organized a conference of these historians from a number of countries, to be held at Pomona College in the early 80's. The College, suddenly realizing with horror what kind of a conference it would be hosting, only got out of their contract on the technicality that McCalden had used the name "Lewis Brandon" on the application forms.[3]

McCalden first appeared on the library scene when he discovered that the Torrance Public Library, in California, was about to put up a "Banned Books Week" display in April, 1984. This display, sponsored by the Office for Intellectual Freedom of the American Library Association, takes place in libraries all over the country at that season, and includes titles frequently found on lists of books which communities have tried to make libraries remove from their shelves. Such titles include: *The adventures of Huckleberry Finn, Go ask Alice, To kill a mockingbird,* and *The diary of Anne Frank*—this last, because (among other reasons) there are those who believe the diary is a hoax. Indeed, one of the books distributed by McCalden is *The hoax of the twentieth century,* which "proves" that the diary is written with a ballpoint pen. Since ballpoints did not come into use until after the World War II, the claim is made that the diary is a fake. As I understand it, the diary came into the hands of Anne Frank's uncle, who merely went over Anne's penciled writing with a ballpoint pen, to make it easier to publish.

McCalden approached the Torrance Public Library with an offer to augment the exhibit with books he was distributing, including the *Hoax* book, plus others he claimed have been banned, or their authors fired, in European countries where freedom of the press is more restricted than in the United States. Initially rebuffed, then stalled, in Torrance, McCalden approached the American Library Association's Office for Intellectual Freedom, where apparently director Judith Krug referred him to the Intellectual Freedom Committee of the California Library Association, chaired by Peter Mollema. The Association's executive director, Stefan B. Moses, himself a refugee from the Holocaust, attended the spring meeting of the committee which discussed the McCalden case. The committee did not vote to support McCalden, but we (I was on the committee) did not take a strong stand against him either; so we were all relieved when Moses said he would offer to let McCalden have a booth at the November CLA conference. Later, a southern California group of librarians offered to sponsor McCalden's appearance on a panel on banned books in general (without necessary reference to his collection). Under the rules then prevailing at CLA conferences, any person or group staffing a booth or table in the exhibits area was allowed to conduct a program in the meeting rooms, by reserving space and time with CLA headquarters. The CLA Intellectual Freedom Committee, and perhaps others, expressed confidence that Moses and CLA President Bernard Kreissman (University of California, Davis), would be able to handle any crisis that might arise out of the appearance of so controversial a speaker.

As it happened, however, a librarian "leaked" the information to the Anti-Defamation League in Los Angeles, and this group induced Moses to cancel the program. The California Library Association's attorneys then warned Moses that he faced a lawsuit if he broke the contract, so he reinstated the program. As the November conference drew near, the CLA headquarters telephone was busy with inquiries and protests, while Moses and the Los Angeles City Police devised a plan to protect the Hotel Bonaventure from disruptions allegedly planned (by survivors' groups and others) to protest McCalden's appearance. The Los Angeles City Council refused to support the California Library Association and prevented Los Angeles City Library System librarians from attending the conference on company time. Finally, when the police indicated that they would be unable to protect the hotel as planned (possibly because of the scheduled appearance of a major rock concert star that same night, elsewhere in town), Moses and Kreissman finally cancelled the program (16 November 1984). The California Library Association and the Los Angeles City Council sent each other resolutions of reproof; the members of CLA indulged in divisive recriminations, and McCalden himself appeared and asked to speak to the plenary session. Finding that no one would sponsor him (for he was not a member), he withdrew. His suit against CLA was finally dismissed in the courts, and Moses retired the next year.[4]

The McCalden incident opened many breaches in the California Library Association which (it was felt at the time) might never be healed. However, although the incident is now sealed in the Association's past, it did challenge librarians to think anew, and thoroughly, the problems of the defense of intellectual freedom.

John Swan, then of Wabash College, Crawfordsville, Indiana, but now director of Bennington College Library in Vermont, published an article, "Untruth or consequences," in *Library journal*.[5] He alluded to the California Library Association's adventures with David McCalden, making the point that CLA's "waffling had the virtue of self-examination, and it is doubtful whether any similar organization would have behaved differently under the circumstances"[6] I replied to him in an article, "Cardinal Mazarin is dead?!," in *Sipapu*.[7]

Correspondence with John Swan led to my challenging him to a debate at the American Library Association's conference in New Orleans. His paper was entitled "Lies, damned lies, and democracy," while mine was "Truth, libraries, and revolution." With Kathleen Heim (Louisiana State University) in the chair, the audience gave 76 votes to Swan, 26 to Peattie, and 26 thought we were both mad. The conversation was quite stimulating—the names of Gramsci and Wittgenstein were tossed about the room—and the loser took the winner to dinner, as the challenge specified.

Even given this background it may not be easy to understand why one audience member, Robert Franklin of McFarland & Company, Inc., Publishers, prodded both of us into revising our papers into essays suitable for publication. For me, at least, the question pierces a problem perennial among librarians: Is freedom our kind of truth, or is truth prior to freedom? Must we distinguish, at some point or level, between "true" texts, and "false" ones, or should we not try to make this distinction and simply provide access to the widest variety of materials (within limits of budget and time), and let the public make up its mind as to the value of such materials, competing in the "free marketplace of ideas"? What is the moral responsibility of librarians for highly controversial materials in their collections? And how do we deal with the person who demands free speech for groups holding theories, which, if they prevailed in the body politic, would diminish or destroy free speech? Are the traditional defenses of intellectual freedom, as they are taught in the profession, adequate to defend us against those who misrepresent historical or scientific fact? Old questions, hashed over by philosophers since Plato. Rarely, however, have they been probed in a library context—the heart of information and culture in a contemporary society. When librarians talk about intellectual freedom, they usually indulge in "platform speeches" ringing with well-intentioned (and widely credited) platitudes. This paper intends to probe more deeply into librarianship's most cherished assumptions and defenses.

II.

Before embarking on this enterprise I must get some problems out of the way. First, to say that intellectual freedom is ill-defended is not to dismiss intellectual freedom as not worth defending. If librarians are divided on questions such as those the "revisionists" offer, that does not mean that they are cherishing an illusory freedom, or that "bourgeois freedoms" are illusory in general. Rather, it does mean that when they do reach a decision, they will (sometimes) need stronger reasons for reaching it than those commonly taught in the profession and its schools.

A second problem lies in the nature of truth, and competing theories of truth, with attendant questions such as the "liar's paradox," and problems purely philosophical in nature. I shall be less interested in these than in the nature of the limits of toleration, and the effects that untruths have in the larger society, with some attention to the responsibility of intellectual workers (such as librarians) in a society like ours. I will touch only on the pragmatic theory of truth, since I believe it has some relation to the foundations of current library practice, — without necessarily attaching such a theory to any particular librarian, including John Swan.

A third problem, raised by several readers of the debate version of this paper, is whether a historical revisionist, such as McCalden, or even a Nazi or neo–Nazi, is deliberately propagating a falsehood, or is simply a pathological person with a bizarre desire to believe something that isn't so — namely, that the Holocaust didn't happen. Are we dealing, therefore, with a "con man," or with someone who is just "mixed up"? Is it not unfair to make assumptions about the "revisionist"'s motives, and should we not simply dismiss them as harmless nuts whom the public will easily see through?

I am inclined to think of this problem as a false one, since McCalden has described himself as a racist[8], and in any case, the consistent utterance of a belief which is not true eventually convinces the utterer himself that the statement he is uttering is true; the deceiver becomes the deceived. Rather than psychoanalyze McCalden, or Hitler, I would offer the case of Joshua Norton, a.k.a.

Norton the First, Emperor of the United States and Protector of Mexico (1819-1880). Whether this deluded and bankrupt little man really believed that he was what he said he was, when all of San Francisco, even crowned heads abroad, pretended to go along with him, we shall never know (Norton's tombstone, in Colma, gives no hint of his original name). The differences between the irritable, peppery, but harmless Norton, and the charming, but serious McCalden, seem plain (to me, at least, though I was born over fifty years too late to meet His Imperial Majesty). McCalden's conferences were well funded; Norton begged dimes and nickels "for the Imperial Treasury." McCalden has an ideology, a "theme," to offer; Norton had no one but himself. McCalden has followers — Norton had only fellow-players in his game of make-believe. Finally, Norton threatened no one, while the Holocaust "revisionists" threaten the identity of Jews the world over.[9]

A person, with whatever motives, who denies the reality (however qualified) of the Holocaust of the Jews and other victims, stands (in my thinking) in a different catalog of "untruth-tellers" than other people. Swan admits this in saying, "antisemitism is a disease not like every one else's diseases."

The reason for this is that the history of the Jews, in their minds, at least, stands in a different position to their present than that of many (but surely not all) other people. Their Scripture, as accepted among them and also by Christians (and, less explicitly, by Moslems), describes their covenants with God. Their history, beginning shortly before the Common Era, describes their sufferings under the hands of Gentile peoples in the Diaspora. To describe any part of that history, including the period of their last and greatest suffering, as false, is not merely to question a statistic, but to attempt to brainwash a population — to commit a kind of "genocide by false history."

Let me take this a step further: among most Americans, history is the province of scholars, and of a few "buffs" — people who can tell you just where Kearny was when he was killed at Chantilly, or just why and where USS *Northampton* was sunk by the Japanese. Among other peoples — including Jews, blacks, Amerindians, women, colonized or lately-colonized people — history is the story of their survival. From their point of view, which I frankly adopt, attempts to rewrite history, however pled for under the excuse of "free speech," are simply attempts to re-enslave them. As for the defense by pathology argument, I concede that while motives may be beyond scrutiny, actions are not. Actions are visible; actions have consequences. Put it crudely, and judge a "street emperor" by this criterion: does he request a dime for his treasury, or does he seek your life, or those of your neighbors? For though McCalden does not demand lives — only a hearing — there is no predicting where a self-identified racist will stop.

III.

I would prefer, instead, to examine my taxonomy of texts, which includes books, periodicals, ephemera, audiovisual materials — the whole range of wordage that a library might have — by the amount of truth or falsity that may lie within them.

In recognizing that this is not the only criterion for acquiring texts, I must make plain, first, what I deem to lie outside this taxonomy. I exclude, at one sweep, all fiction, and much of the world of belles-lettres — I banish hence all weekend essayists, from Addison to Norman Cousins; I set the Bible and its critics on one side, also jeremiads and exhortations to repentance, prophecies of doom, divinations, advices from Mother; all love letters, excuses, rationalizations, tomes of casuistry; letters to the Editor, challenges to duels, apologies "the morning after"; books of Hindu philosophy printed on gray paper, books written "as told to" or transmitted through a "channel"; all "treasuries" of *anything;* all discount catalogs, all requests for money other than personal — but these last shade into a category which I *will* discuss, and which will surprise the reader with its hearty, coarse, but irresistible, appearance.

Professional librarians, worried over intellectual freedom, may be confronted with a number of different forms of controversial expression, of which these are the most obvious (learned colleagues are invited to distinguish, or to unite, or both):

1. Mathematical and logical truths ($2 + 2 = 4$; p cannot imply not-p)
2. Empirical truths (the Earth is round [roundish])
3. Opinions, on which people may honestly differ (Republicans, Democrats, a third party, left or right)
4. Matters of taste: J.S. Bach, or ZZ Top?
5. Moral questions: abortion, homosexuality, right or wrong?
6. Minority theories or opinions, not generally accepted by scholars in the field, but carrying no extra moral or political weight, no

hidden agenda: Bacon wrote Shakespeare's plays, the Air Force has a flying saucer and its occupants in a refrigerator at Travis Air Force Base, Fairfield, California

7. Offensive language (which cannot, *per se,* be true or false, save under the broadest political view; this includes four-letter words, racist epithets, pornography)
8. Bullshit (a word of which the definition will appear later)
9. Outright lies, false statements knowingly made to mislead, frighten, or hurt people (black people are ineducable, the Holocaust didn't happen)

Not all of these are on the same kind of truth-spectrum; some, like no. 7, are outside it. However, all of these texts in my taxonomy (books, periodicals, whatever) are apt to be texts of controversy with which librarians must be prepared to deal. In numbers 5, 6, 8, and 9, at least, there is a strong truth-or-falsity component. (With 5, for example: is rock music satanist in origin, or in eventual effect?) Librarians have met all of these texts with the *Library Bill of Rights,* and with careful selection tools. Librarians have even met with a new awareness of community concern; the Library of Congress, for instance, changed at least some of the offensive subject headings, which I would list under no. 7; though at the very least, peoples (including African peoples) should be listed under their own names.

But in general, these defenses, while adequate for the first six, where the profession's libertarian attitude is understood and supported by the populace — have not fared well with no. 7, and have (I submit) failed completely with numbers 8 and 9.

There is, however, a spectrum, however broken or inadequately stated, of truth or falsity, from beginning to end in this taxonomy. Librarians have been accustomed to approach all these texts, answering all these descriptions, on the basis of the following criteria:

1. Access (is at least some access [local or nearly so] available for this material?)
2. Need (are patrons asking for it? Is the demand simply prompted by a television special, or is demand recurrent throughout the seasons?)
3. Cost (can it be leased, or must it be purchased?)
4. Time (is there enough demand to warrant staff hours assembling a collection, of whatever scope and size, in this field?)

5. Relevance (is it closely connected to existing local collections?)
6. Permanent value: the product of all of these factors (with especial weight given to 2, 3, and 5)

    Librarians dealing with these nine controversial texts, may apply any one or all of the six criteria, without ever asking themselves, "is this text true, or false?" Of course, the librarian in her daily round may indeed use personal knowledge, even frankly acknowledged personal inclination, in deciding whether or not to decide to introduce the "text" to the collection, or even the speaker to the state library association. She may *know,* in short, that the UFO and its alien occupants are *not* at Travis Air Force Base in Fairfield, California, but at Lackland AFB, San Antonio, Texas. My point is that the librarian may choose to admit this "truth," or she may choose to ignore it, in her assessment of the materials to be added to the library.

    The passage (on tape) that Stefan Moses played (at a follow-up the next spring)[11] from the proceedings of the Los Angeles City Council, included the voice of one Council member who said that libraries, which ought to be the repositories of truth, should not contain a falsehood. Of course, as Judith Sessions (then of California State University, Chico) pointed out, libraries contain a great deal more than just truths: they contain the different kinds of texts I have listed, plus the ones I have banished from discussion (fiction, poetry, etc.), and doubtless many more. Whether they should also collect books embodying lies (women are not equal to men, there was no Holocaust)—except in the case of omnivorous research collections: or whether library associations should promote such books, their authors and publishers—is unsettled at this point, as far as the profession is concerned.

    Some librarians trained in the present libertarian tradition of intellectual freedom might say, "Buy the book but don't promote it." Others would say, "That's a cop-out. If you don't believe it, why get it?" But no librarian, as librarian (and not as citizen), will be found publicly saying, "That book is a lie." To say that, would be to reveal oneself as close-minded, intolerant, afraid of new or controversial ideas; rude to the author, the reader, perhaps to the little cult around the corner. Whether the librarian is speaking on the job or off, she runs the same risk (at least in some communities). Acquire the book, then, with the broad proclamation: "We collect all materials and cover a wide variety of opinions, no matter how offensive to some, since freedom for what we want implies, nay includes, freedom for the detestable."

A more candid construction would be, ". . . freedom for that which we, personally and collectively, detest." The quote is never given in just that way, perhaps because it would raise the questions, who are "we"? and what are our reasons? Do some people know more than others, have suffered more than others? And should the librarian be hearkening to such people?

Of course, while all sides of a controversy may be represented in the library, the librarian's position of neutrality may be restricted to collection policy only. Collecting, and believing (or judging) may be, and can be, two different things, at least in the librarian's mind. (And of course one may collect neutrally on a subject or issue, but for reasons other than impartiality's sake: curriculum support, for example.) A text, finally need not be a lie to be preposterous: see controversial· opinion number 6 (Bacon versus Shakespeare, e.g.). Indeed, the preposterous may actually be enjoyable — witness the space-alien literature, or the grocery-newsstand tabloids. The lie is that which sickens and offends, and that is why including the "detestable" in the category of a library's desiderata, while sometimes defensible, always raises grave questions.

Asked therefore, by a student whether a book which denies the reality of the Holocaust, is "true or not," the cautious librarian, adhering to the strictest tradition of neutrality, might use the dodge of "Read it, read some other material over here, and make up your own mind!" Or, as writers of biology textbooks, approaching the subject of evolution, begin, "Some scholars think. . ." or even (here we're getting bold!) "Many knowledgeable scholars think. . . ." Of course, it seems unlikely that any librarian would make that remark to a reader; but at least some of the language of the profession implies such noncommittal attitudes.

However, the public does, after all, trust us, as the "libraries should not contain falsehoods" remark (however naive) of the Los Angeles City Councilman suggests, and pays us accordingly. The public understands that we have to be equitable; but it requires that we be honest. They will not tolerate our pretending suddenly that we don't know something, when the rest of the time we seem to know everything else. While it is true that the lie that the Holocaust didn't happen has spread in some communities (one reason that *The diary of Anne Frank* sometimes appears on banned book lists), there are too many survivors, plus Allied military personnel and civilian rescue workers, who saw the camps just after they were liberated, to let us pretend that the Holocaust was a myth, a theory, or even just a minor operation.

If this is true, then a crack appears at the very foundations of our beliefs and practices in the domain of intellectual freedom. We practice information science, yet there are times when we dare not say that the information before us is inaccurate, bigoted, or misleading (deliberately or no). Either we know, or do not know, however, *some* matters of fact: those witnessed and suffered by millions. We can admit that there are some areas on which we lack sufficient information to judge: but this terrible episode is not one of them.

"Librarians don't know anything, they just know where to look it up." This statement would more nearly approach the real state of our profession, if for "anything," we substitute "everything." (Even so, there are things we don't know where to look up; we surprise ourselves on the job every day). Still, thousands of librarians, in libraries academic, public and special, are experts in their fields, and are so treated, consulted, and rewarded. They have the facts as well as the bibliographical references. They *do* know; and we know: about the Holocaust. *It happened: why pretend?*

When I first wrote an earlier version of these words on neutrality, I felt a certain discomfort in imagining that any librarian would actually balance Holocaust studies with Holocaust "revisionist" works.[12] This has actually happened. Edmonton Public Library, Alberta, accepted some 150 Holocaust-related titles from the Jewish Federation of Edmonton, and then went out and acquired the revisionist titles most requested by patrons. Cataloging is not reported to reflect the revisionist nature of these works; *Is the diary of Anne Frank genuine?* is assigned the subject headings FRANK, ANNE, and JEWS – NETHERLANDS – BIOGRAPHY, although the Library of Congress lists the subject heading HOLOCAUST, JEWISH – ERRORS, INVENTIONS, ETC.[13]

What may have prompted Edmonton Public Library is unclear. Apparently a teacher in Alberta has been on trial for making "revisionist" statements (in class?). There are antiracist laws in Canada, as in the United Kingdom; they do not have our broadly written First Amendment. In that case the Edmonton Public Library could defend its action as simply giving the public access to these materials, in order to see what the fuss was about. They might even build up a collection on the subject – as the Simon Wiesenthal people have — *they* displayed McCalden's books at the CLA conference. Still, the way they handled the subject headings makes one wonder whether they quite knew what they were doing. The Jewish Federation did not think that the Edmonton Public Library people knew what they were doing: according to the report cited, they were outraged.

IV.

Swan's *Library journal* article, "Untruth or consequences,"[14] reprinted in this book, was for me the catalyst that started this whole debate. While not the sole text I now have from him, I find here my greatest distance from my colleague, and wish to analyze it as closely as possible.[14]

"Truth," says Swan, "is the most precious commodity in the information market for practical as well as idealistic reasons — the 'truth' here being that of Mill, Milton, and Socrates, not the far more common reason, which Ambrose Bierce defined as an 'ingenious compound of desirability and appearance'" (*Lj,* p. 44).

It could of course be argued, that Bierce had the advantage over Mill and Milton (though not over Socrates) of undergoing combat experience, and therefore had a better understanding of nineteenth-century news reports, but then this would have made Bierce more of a skeptic than either Swan or myself. Swan does indeed refer to the McCalden case (*Lj,* p. 46–49), and his point is that as librarians, our cause is not truth, but freedom.

> The commitment of librarians as an absolute legal defense should never be confused with our basic professional commitment to the flow of all kinds of information without regard to its truth or falsehood. Truth may be, must be, an absolute defense under the law, but it has no such place in the selection, classification, storage, and weeding decisions made by librarians [Swan, *Lj,* p. 46; the illustration on p. 45 of the original article is itself *illustrative*].

Of course, we can all assume that a mathematical text in error due to a glitch in a computer, is to be weeded out on discovery. The question of $2 + 2 = 4$ is not up for grabs. Old issues of the *Physicians' desk reference* may also be weeded *sans* hesitation, surely. Again, the real world offers us a multiplicity of "truths" compounded of desirability and appearance, often contradictory, sometimes in violent conflict with one another. As human beings we inevitably hold cause with one or many of these truths, but as librarians our cause is, in a very practical sense, not truth but freedom. Indeed, our truth *is* freedom, freedom of access, freedom for our patrons to draw upon our resources, to sort their own truths out of our carefully collected melange of truths, half-truths, untruths, and nontruths [Swan, *Lj*, p. 46].

Is it a melange? Even a melange requires some sorting; but let us not be unfair. . . These noble words, to which most librarians would agree, conceal a few problems. The real world does not "offer" us anything; the universe is not a radio station, broadcasting opinions: it simply *is*. The multiplicity of statements to which Swan refers, is not the world: "Don't confuse the finger pointing at the moon with the moon itself." The librarian, in collecting this melange, can only hope, not know, that the reader has enough education, patience, and discernment, to engage in the sorting process and come out with the "right" answer. But even educated people have their prejudices; you can hear them at any Faculty Club.

Without criticizing the California Library Association, or Stefan B. Moses, or (at all!) supporting the views attributed to McCalden, Swan concludes that "We are committed both to the search for truth and for the freedom of expression of untruth" (*Lj*, p. 49), although he admits that "many people are ready to grant the untruth some theoretical place in the network of free debate, but no place that will somehow grant that place legitimacy" (p. 49).

Swan further makes a distinction between "intellectual freedom" and his own position: "We are not defending the presence of untruth in our libraries just because it might turn out to be true. McCalden's arguments will never turn out to be true, and 'Creation science' will always turn out to be apologetics masquerading as empiricism, but both have a place in our libraries" (*Lj*, p. 50; he does not say how he would classify them, or what subject headings he would assign them). He concludes with this point: "The knowledge of truth and the knowledge of untruth, like the knowledge of good and evil, are indissolubly joined. Our cause, professionally and politically, is with both of them" (p. 52).

Swan, bless him, does have the humanity of inconsistency:

We do indeed bring our own versions of truth to the job. We don't put them behind us when we make professional judgments. Selection and weeding and organizing and providing access and guidance are all carried out with at least one eye cocked on the truth, or at least a consensus thereof established by the review media, public opinion, and other measures. We prefer to buy books that tell the truth about life or dog grooming or history or solar panels, rather than those which distort, mislead, lie, or just make mistakes [Swan, *Lj,* p. 47].

It is important to note that here Swan deviates from the pure libertarian position on intellectual freedom, for he takes up the confusion often observed between those who state a fact and those who state a moral opinion *as if it were* a fact: "There are a lot of people who *know* that abortion is murder, and some of them liken abortion-on-demand to the Holocaust. They are about as interested in maintaining an open forum on the subject as most of us are interested in debating the Nazis" (*Lj,* p. 47–49). A debate about abortion is a moral debate; a debate about the Holocaust, if we are talking about the number of victims, is purely factual, although there are certainly moral implications—the main reason I object to the presence of McCalden at a library conference. Here, it appears, Swan and I disagree, for the whole middle section of his article, describing the McCalden encounter with the California Library Association, strongly suggests that it would have seemed better to him had McCalden been allowed to speak.

Two statements of fact, which happen to be false, may also have, or have not, moral implications: "The Earth is flat" and "The Holocaust didn't happen." The first is morally weightless, as so stated, while the second is loaded with moral, social, and political implications. (It could be objected that there might be some dangerous flat-earthers, but the only one I can think of is Wilbur Glenn Voliva, and even he only tried to rule Zion, Illinois.[15])

To put the above-quoted statements in the same category as the utterances of kooks whom we may tolerate, because in the "free marketplace of ideas" both will be tolerated, is not to think historically, and therefore not to think clearly. The "Earth is flat" statement has not been accepted for many years. The second appears to be believed, to some extent, and with some modifications of detail, by a number of people: a collection of minorities, some of whom, if they secured wide acceptance of their ideas, might get into power and thereby establish a condition of things in which the "free marketplace of ideas" would be suppressed.[16]

The first statement is one of Swan's "untruths"; but the second statement, quoted above, is a *lie*.

I define a *lie* as a falsehood deliberately uttered to deceive and hurt people, by a person who really knows the truth but deliberately denies or distorts it. (This excludes people with a passionate need to believe something that they know, or half-know, or partially or secretly deny, something that in their "heart of hearts" [by definition, beyond the scope of this essay] they "know" to be true; it therefore excludes Norton, Voliva, alcoholics, the whole genus of those who are [at least, borderline] mentally ill.) This concept is not deeply explored in Swan's paper, nor in many other places.

There are some cases in which the law takes cognizance of a lie: if I write a check for a sum greater than my bank account, I am guilty of a felony, and the basic assumption here is that I have lied in stating that I had funds sufficient to cover the amount for which I wrote the check. Again, if I write a false statement which damages another person, I am liable at law; though in the first case the law invoked against me is criminal, the second is civil. In each case, however, a malicious falsehood is at the base of the prosecution. In each case, I did something which (intentionally or otherwise) deceived another person.

What troubles me, however, is that statement (source? I'm unable to trace it!): "If you say that one woman is a slut, she can sue you. If you say that all women are sluts, *they* have no recourse at law nor in equity." How does this apply to libraries, books held by libraries, people who might be invited to library associations?

Again, the question of sincerity is raised: a critic of the debate version of this paper wrote, "I believe there is some reason to believe that Hitler was sincere, not the knave, in his antisemitism." My best answer to this is that (by no means!) was Hitler the first antisemite. Indeed, he was only the latest. Antisemitism, like other forms of xenophobia the world around, had been prevalent in Central Europe for generations. Hitler simply "kicked the tires, and bought the car." From the point of view of his victims, does it matter whether he was sincere, or insincere; whether he came early, or late, to his beliefs; whether he was an inventor, or follower, of previous phobias; indeed, whether he believed in astrology, or not?

Having eliminated these objections, may we not describe Swan's word "untruth" as a euphemism? He tells us (*Lj,* p. 52) that "we must make it clear to our public that access means a professional responsibility to . . . as much untruth as we can possibly manage."

Perhaps there is room for another concept; that of the Big Lie. First in our century applied to Jews, earlier applied to Jews, blacks, women, many other people: the Big Lie — tell it often enough, loud enough, demand equal time for it, buy up advertising space for it, until you win! — is this "untruth": that there is a group of people who are "sub-human," who are "the cause of all the trouble in this world," and who therefore are fair game: it's *all right* to push them around, to discriminate against them, and finally — if someone gives the right orders — to exterminate them. In this country it applies to minorities; women are assaulted by men who believe in women's inferiority. The Big Lie, believed by a whole nation and by many outside it, caused the deaths of six million Jews: *because they were Jews:* and not because they had done anything.

The Big Lie has not been absent from our own country. It has been most visibly present in the struggle to liberate black Americans first from slavery, later from discrimination. But perhaps there is room for a Big Truth: there are no subhuman people, and (finally) Truth cannot endure the presence of a Lie. It has to fight the Lie, and overcome it. The Lie (which lay behind the rationalization of segregation) had to be destroyed first by the Civil War; later by the civil rights movement. The Rev. Dr. Martin Luther King, Jr., was led to oppose the lie of racism with the truth that was in him.

Herzstein, in describing the success of Hitler's propaganda with the German people, explains why he has no separate chapter on anti-Jewish propaganda:

> Anti-Jewish feeling permeated every level of the Nazi propaganda apparatus and mass media, even after the Nazis had "evacuated" millions of Jews to the east. Since the enemy coalition was clearly a conspiracy, the arch-conspirator, the Jew, was portrayed as the mind behind the "anti-world." The Jews were responsible for German misery and German defeats. To have a chapter on the Jews would be to acknowledge anti-Semitism as a part of Nazi ideology, whereas it was its ultimate moral and historical guide.[17]

Before going on to examine the foundations of the libertarian theory I would like to share with you my discovery of a new kind of "text," which constitutes a new item to the list of texts I originally published in *Sipapu,*[18] and reproduced on pages 41–42 above. This is no. 8, bullshit. I discovered Harry G. Frankfurt's essay "On bull-shit"[19] purely by chance (while working in our library's standing order approval plan: an excellent reason to let librarians read on the job), and discovered that this British philosopher is about the only person who has written on this subject, although he refers to a book by Max Black, *On humbug,* which I have not read. He quotes Black's definition of humbug as deceptive misrepresentation short of lying, especially by pretentious word or deed, of somebody's own thoughts, feelings, or attitudes (Frankfurt, p. 118).

Frankfurt also adds to the above definition of Black's a certain slovenliness, mindlessness; not a willful disregard for truth, but a disregard for the truth-value of what the speaker says, that charac-terizes the speaker as uttering bullshit. Bullshit need not be false: it is immaterial whether the statement uttered by the bullshitter is true or false. What does matter is the bullshitter's hidden agenda:

> The bullshitter may not deceive us, or even intend to do so, either about the facts or what he takes them to be. What he does neces-sarily attempt to deceive us about is his enterprise. His only in-dispensably distinctive characteristic is that in a certain way he misrepresents what he is up to [Frankfurt, p. 131].

Others may judge whether or not I misrepresent Frankfurt: The honest man pays his debt when due; the liar tells you he paid you last Thursday (and knows perfectly well that he did not); the bull-shitter tells you that he will pay you when his rich uncle's ship comes in. The uncle, and the ship, may exist, or may not exist; they might just as well have been made up on the spur of the moment.

This raises anew the status of the "revisionist historians." Are they liars, or simply bullshitters? Lest we take comfort from the lat-ter possibility, and dismiss them as harmless cranks, let us listen to Frankfurt once again:

> For this reason, telling lies does not tend to unfit a person for telling the truth in the same way that bullshitting does. Through excessive indulgence in the latter activity, which involves making assertions without paying any attention to anything except what it suits one to say, a person's normal habit of attending to the way things are may become attenuated or lost. Someone who lies and someone who tells the truth are playing on opposite sides, so to speak, in the same game. Each responds to the facts as he understands them, although

the responsibility of the one is guided by the authority of the truth, while the other defies that authority and refuses to meet its demands. The bullshitter ignores these demands altogether. He does not reject the authority of the truth, as the liar does, and oppose himself to it. He pays no attention to it at all. By virtue of this, bullshit is a greater enemy of the truth than lies are" [Frankfurt, p. 132].

The purpose of this digression is to illustrate the variety of possible alternatives to the truth (mathematical, or scientific) that may confront the librarian working with texts or inviting speakers. Granted the librarian's own frailty — and if there are few liars, there are plenty of eccentrics and not a few bullshitters in our noble profession — the librarian must always have an eye cocked for the truth, in Swan's phrase, in his own daily copings. One may or may not agree with Frankfurt that the bullshitter is more dangerous than the liar; I would suppose it depends on context, on how easily they may be found out. Certainly I would be unable to appeal to any universal standard of truth, any miraculous touchstone, by which such detection might be eased. Nor can I advocate a "party line" to which all must hew. The only appeal I shall be making in these pages is to the librarian's personal decency, to the profession's collective honor.

V.

Given this diversity of opinions, truths, half-truths, and untruths with which the librarian must cope, how can she find a theory, a substrate, to sort and understand the melange? In some regards, the theory of librarianship resembles (though it has never claimed any descent from, and Swan does not mention) the pragmatic theory of truth, as promulgated by John Dewey. For the pragmaticists in the truth-question, truth emerges as the result of a search: an investigation which begins in doubt and uncertainty, and ends with the establishment of a *fact*. The fact, or truth, has no prior existence; its existence depends on the corroboration of supporting facts by ordered inquiry.[20] Or, put more crudely, that theory is truest which works best; the Earth was proved round by circumnavigation, not by speculation.

Since this process requires a free investigator, and since there are many investigators, there will be many facts (about the same problem); and many interpretations of those facts. Truth, therefore (yours, mine, McCalden's) will become harder to pin down: it becomes a concept more mutable, more discussable—alas, more evanescent?

For many librarians, this will be the ultimate victory—even for those who do not call themselves pragmatists, pragmaticists, or any other variation of the word. They have, after all, budgets to balance and crazies to appease, and theoretical foundations interest them less than that of the foundations of Heaven. I for one, can't blame them; getting through the daily round is hard enough even if you are the sole librarian in a church library (which, on weekends, I am), with a small budget and an indulgent readership.

I can only applaud such librarians who, working with the *Library Bill of Rights,* and with minimal support from school boards or county supervisors, battle hordes of weirdos who emerge from the woodwork to demand the removal of books from a prescribed list which the librarian may, or may not, have ever heard of. To support such librarians is my reason for renewing my annual membership in the Freedom to Read Foundation. However, I hesitate when I am asked to encourage the appearance at a library conference, of a person who, insulting the Jews by denying an important and undeniably tragic fact of their history, is admitted to a panel to speak on "banned books" without any definite idea of what he might bring up in his bibliography.

I am suggesting that the librarian does have a responsibility to "stay sane": to be able, and to help the community to be able, to distinguish truth from falsehood, allowable opinion from bigoted manipulation, eccentricity from unworthy ambition. The librarian, like other intellectual workers, has a responsibility to the culture of her country, beyond passive access.

"Freedom for what we like includes freedom for what we detest; for freedom is indivisible." This is so often quoted in library literature, that I venture nobody knows its source (I don't). This quotation, for me, however, raises more questions than it answers. Going back to an earlier point: Detestable for what reasons, and to whom? Is everything we detest to be included on our shelves? Certainly not; no librarian would go out and buy the stock of an "adult" bookstore to prove the point. Are two people, with two different detestations, of equal weight, and are their complaints to merit equal courtesy or disregard? Is a lady who finds a naughty word in a book just as important as a Jew who objects to a racist speaker? What are the reasons, what are the motivations of these two complainers? Does the Jew know something that the librarians don't know, or may have chosen to ignore?

Is freedom indivisible? Who said it was? If it is indivisible, what principle of unity holds it together? In law and custom, there are many restraints on freedom, including freedom of speech (I shall get to those when I consider Schauer's book). I am not setting out to prove that freedom *is* divisible; I am merely suggesting that librarians repeat these shibboleths to each other without any real thought of their origin or possible implications.

Another shibboleth: In the free marketplace of ideas, all false ideas will eventually be *proved* false, and if the free market is allowed to operate freely, the good ideas will be accepted, and the bad ones rejected, by popular wisdom and common understanding. I must make clear at the outset that neither this nor the previous defense is necessarily that of John Swan. Swan himself has criticized the "free marketplace of ideas," but the phrase is so frequently employed in library literature that the idea "there is a free marketplace of ideas" is too easily (by some librarians) conflated with the idea "the free marketplace of ideas is a Good Thing." Of course, the two ideas are not the same. In fact, some people would support this counter-idea: "Yes, *at present* there may be a free marketplace of ideas, but I don't think it's a Good Thing, I think it's a Bad Thing, and I intend to use this freedom to subvert the market, and replace it with my own ideology. And if anybody tries to stop me, I'll say that he is a censor, and so turn his own defenses against him."

Swan quotes (*Lj,* p. 52) a disappointed McCalden as having said "there is no free speech in America." Of course, as Swan points out, McCalden is wrong, but not just because it is empirically untrue: we can cite many examples of censorship and silenced speech, among ourselves as librarians, in society, by government — some of which we admit to, some of which we don't talk about, some of which we gladly permit and some of which we strenuously oppose. McCalden is wrong when he takes the fact that no one was willing to sponsor him as a speaker at the membership meeting of the California Library Association as a proof of the statement that there is no free speech in America; he makes his particular case to be the proof of a general condition. This is an elementary logical fallacy; but how many librarians, assuming the indivisibility of freedom of speech, make the same mistake?

This is not to say that we should not rally to the defense of books banned and librarians fired; but rather that we should consider cases on their own merits. Nor is it an abandonment of principle to decline to hear every speaker who comes to our platforms. We live, after all, in the real world—not Voliva's—and it will not suddenly "go flat" for us if we change our minds about listening to an avowed racist.

VI.

It might be useful at this point to get away from the philosophers and summon the aid of a practicing historian. Oscar Handlin in *Truth in history* (1979) demolishes William Appleton Williams's *Contours in American history* (1961). For Handlin, Williams's error is that of a "revisionist" view from the left, which blames the Cold War entirely on the United States.

> The revisionists did not recognize or explain away their distortions. Instead, they justified error by further abuse of the evidence and put in question the very integrity of history as a discipline . . . the revisionists and their defenders confused public opinion at a time when clarity on these issues was important; and they did serious damage to scholarship.[21]

Handlin points out that even the learned can be dishonest:

> Every profession that claims immunity from outside interference and freedom of expression for its members must recognize self-regulating, self-correcting procedures to catch out the crooks, plagiarists and fools. History is no more free of knaves than other fields. No science is devoid of the cooked-up experiment, the misallocated funds, the blunders that are products of stupidity. The important question is, what is done when the fault is discovered? [Handlin, p. 157]. . . .
> Meanwhile, imperturbable, indefatigable William Appleton Williams continued to set fantasy in print to the bafflement of librarians who still gave his books non-fiction classifications [Handlin, p. 161].[22]

Here, of course, Handlin offers us librarians a challenge beyond our rights and powers. Most of us supposed Williams to be no more than a respected radical historian: his errors of fact only a major scholar like Handlin could detect. We have no choice but to accept Williams's books as history, classify them as such, place Handlin's alongside them, and hope that the student of history will come to his own best conclusions. If a faculty member, Handlin's criticism in hand, should demand that Williams's book be reclassified to fiction, we would surely be right in refusing him. Aside from the fact that "we can't please everybody," we would be out of order in accepting one scholar's word over another. Still, "our truth *is* freedom" no longer sounds as ringingly as it does in Swan's paper. In the academic circles where both of us move, guiding students is the supreme practice of public service work; and where the librarian is unable to discriminate, the student is liable to err.

Since I myself haven't read Williams, my problem is to decide how much Handlin is correct, and how much is mere fulminating; or putting it the other way around, how much of Williams's work is correct, or half-true, and how much is sinister brainwashing? Of one thing I feel somewhat confident, that Williams is not necessarily trying to deny history in quite the same way that McCalden and his friends are. I don't think that it's true that the United States is wholly to blame for the Cold War (if, indeed, that is what Williams says); but that is entirely different from saying that the Cold War never happened at all. Any record of hostility between two great powers must be fraught with ambiguities; but if the conflict is perceived as conflict, then the conflict happened. On that, surely, all of us can agree.

Williams's book, then, must be retained, and classified as history, because we cannot completely dismiss it as false the way Handlin does. But does this make us more free, or is it a confession of our own (and Handlin's, and Williams's) limitations: of truth, of historical insight? To enlighten us as to the causes of our ambiguous feelings, let me call on Hannah Arendt.

In her essay "Truth and politics"[23] Arendt makes an opposition between the two: politics is the dealing in the marketplace, rational truth is the philosopher's timeless sphere. Factual truth, however is (for Arendt) intimately bound up with politics; it is always in being rewritten and therefore in danger of being destroyed or corrupted: "Facts inform opinions, and opinions, inspired by different interests and passions, can differ widely and still be legitimate truth. Freedom of opinion is a farce unless factual information is not in dispute" (p. 12–13).

Arendt gives us an account of the visit paid by a German scholar, after 1918, to the aging Clemenceau. The German was wondering aloud what historians would say concerning the responsibility for starting the war, and Arendt reports Clemenceau as having replied, "Well, they may say many things, but one thing they won't say, is that Belgium invaded Germany in 1914." We cannot be sure whether Hitler had heard this story when he staged an "invasion" of Polish troops into Germany in 1939, and even in our day there are intellectuals who firmly believe that South Korea invaded North Korea in June 1950. But let us return to Hannah Arendt, for whom truth has an element of coercion: once arrived at, it cannot be changed by majority vote: "The trouble is that factual truth, like all other truth, peremptorily claims to be acknowledged and precludes debate, and debate constitutes the very essence of political life" (p. 15).

For both Handlin and Arendt, therefore, there is a sense of duty to the facts, doubtless common to their lives as historians, that lawyers, philosophers and librarians have difficulty living with. Our liberty, as we see it, runs counter to their scholarship, as they see it. However, while there is obviously a broad area in which facts are uncertain and the truth is in dispute, there are, at least, some boundaries:

> The hallmark of factual truth is that its opposite is neither error, nor illusion, nor opinion, ... but the deliberate falsehood, or lie.... It is clearly an attempt to change the record, and, as such, it is a form of *action*. The same is true when the liar, lacking the power to make his falsehood stick, does not insist on the gospel truth of his statement but pretends that this is his "opinion," to which he has a constitutional right. This is frequently done by subversive groups, and in a politically immature public the resulting confusion can be considerable [Arendt, p. 23].

Several thoughts can be disentangled here. One is that the "constitutional right" of a speaker is not thereby negated. Any McCalden can say what he wants in the streets and squares (while we observe, without legal implications, that in just such localities Hitler got his start). Another is that groups of which history approves — liberators of their several nations, right or left — distort historical or contemporary facts to pursue their own ends. Finally, there is the serious conflict in which both sides reputedly had recourse to self-serving mendacity: this classic case is the Spanish Civil War of 1936–1939. For Thomas, who has gone over all sources, no side is without accounts of atrocities and battles that did or did not take place, casualties inflicted, statistics inflated or deflated as opportunity directed. In cases like these, "access" becomes the only recourse.[24] No doubt, the history of the Vietnamese Conflict will produce similar pros-and-cons, quid-pro-quos, as will the history of the Vietnam War.

Meanwhile, what happened at the California Library Association in November 1984? The last sentence of Arendt's quoted paragraph may be of some help. Arendt makes a further distinction between the old-fashioned political lie (the privilege of statecraft), and the modern manipulation of history for the masses:

> We are finally confronted with highly respected statesmen who, like de Gaulle and Adenauer, have been able to build their basic policies on such evident non-facts as that France belongs among the victors of the last war and hence is one of the great powers, and "that the barbarism of National Socialism had affected only a small percentage of the country" [Arendt, p. 25].

If I understand the historians correctly, they approach truth, freedom, and "the freedom to lie" in a spirit different from the philosophers, librarians and lawyers, to whom I shall return. For historians, truth is imperious, brushing aside fiction and casuistry and demanding that we recognize that the world is round, and that events in it (barring the very obscure, such as the wars of the Picts) really happened: e.g., the Holocaust of the Jews; and that truth is not married to untruth, but is rather married to freedom, under the law of scientific inquiry.

It can be argued, of course, that a librarian is not a historian, and that the librarian's profession is ancillary: to provide historians with the secondary (and sometimes, the primary) sources which they need to compile their works of fact. In this regard it may be necessary to supply them, at least at some research institutions, with works not entirely factual, or about which the librarians have serious doubts. I have done this, surely John Swan has done this; which of us has not? And Handlin's remarks about Williams underscore the difficulties that would face a librarian who would absurdly seek to be a purist in adding works only wholly factual to the collection.

There is such a thing as the history of false history. The reader who wants to investigate a special case of this is invited to read

Bernard Lewis's little book[25] on the fabrication of history among competing states and powers, largely in the Middle East. As new kingships and republics arose, old historical accounts were discarded in accommodation. All documents and claims in this area are therefore suspect. The essays were originally presented at Yeshiva University, but what Bernard Lewis has to say about Masada is not exactly reverent.

What does seem to me clear is that, even if we regard librarians are making available a wider variety of materials than historians, scientists, and other scholars might regard as purely factual, the librarians are still a learned body, and as such, they have a responsibility approximate to the one that Handlin pointed out in his passage on "crooks, plagiarists, and fools." I don't think we have many of those in librarianship: my point is that if we don't have any in our house, we shouldn't associate with any from outside. The spectacle of a group of librarians solemnly sitting and listening to a racist in the name of free speech offends partly because it is naive, but also because it is dishonorable: it contradicts the essential nature of the profession.

It is my understanding that McCalden later addressed the Canadian Library Association, who received him in stony silence. Was this wise? I do not know the exact circumstances under which he spoke, nor how their procedures differed from the ones then prevalent in the California Library Association. Consequently, judgment must be suspended for lack of contextual information. What does seem at least possible is that if McCalden had spoken at *our* library association, we Californians would have never been able to keep silence. A verbal donnybrook would have ensued the minute he began to speak.

For some, this would have been healthier than silence voluntary or enforced, but for me it would still have raised the question, "Why are we associating with this person?" We are not attempting to convert him; we owed him nothing, beyond the terms of the contract; and we did nothing to prevent his spreading his message outside. Indeed, at the next California Library Association conference, in Long Beach, November 1985, McCalden rented a small meeting room in the hotel, held a meeting to oppose the deportation of Nazi war criminals, and placed flyers in the windshields of attendees' cars, urging them to come to court to hear his case decided against CLA. So far as I know, nobody stopped him from distributing his flyers, and nobody went to court to hear him. I attended the meeting for ten minutes just to get a good look at him. I would have objected if anyone had stopped him from distributing his flyers, and would have thought it superfluous to picket his meeting (although it would have been legally permissible). In any case nobody mentioned his presence as a triumph for free speech, or a disgrace to the Association's honor; as long as he was not there under Association auspices, he could be safely ignored. The general feeling seemed to me to be: that's yesterday's problem, let's get on with other things. Which is healthy, providing that we've learned a lesson from the problem.

VII.

Turning now to Swan's documents published in the course of this debate or more recently, I find a lucid thinker aware of the dangers of naive libertarianism. Swan is hard to disagree with because his even style, and elegant command of authorities, makes his position stronger than another writer's restatement of the familiar libertarian view of these matters might be. He avoids the usual defenses of the free marketplace of ideas by pointing out that the marketplace is not always free; some ideas are excluded, some pernicious ideas get circulated, and there is not enough time or opportunity to view the truth at leisure even when it is seen. He does refer to the liberal's paradox, the presence of the advocates of tyranny in the marketplace of liberty, but makes it not a flaw in the argument for the free marketplace, but a necessary condition for the market's freedom.

In his first new essay in this book, "Lies, damned lies, and democracy," Swan derives from Paul Chevigny's *More speech*[26] the following point: we must be able to deal with the defense of our own opinions: if they are questioned, no matter how troubling the question, or how falsely the question is derived, still a question demands an answer. The question may be derived from a widespread popular belief, and that belief must be dealt with. For Swan, imagination and understanding must come into play, when searching for truth, for truth is perceived by individuals, and cannot be dictated to them. Revoking the tenure of professorial "Holocaust revisionists" only creates martyrs for their cause, in the popular mind.

(I find some problems with this last; whether an injured person is regarded as a martyr or a person who richly deserved what he got, depends on popular feeling at the time. When Mary Dyer and three other Quakers were hanged in Boston in 1661, there was a revulsion against this act even among some Puritans, and it moved to executive action the usually frivolous Charles II. When Lyndon La-Rouche was sent to prison a few weeks ago, only a handful of people regretted the sentence — I certainly did not. But martyrology is not my subject. It makes me, — well, *uncomfortable*.)

Swan is, of course, perfectly correct in mentioning popular belief, and when I turn to his page of Chevigny, I find the following quotation, which immediately precedes the quotation that he gives:

> The principle that there can be no predictable limits on discussion leads to the glib conclusion that all opinions must be tolerated. The concrete application of the principle, nevertheless, may still give us pause; as a practical matter it is not very difficult to think of opinions that are unacceptable under any circumstances we can imagine. The most obvious candidate, under the arguments I have made here, is advocacy of a comprehensive system of censorship; another, more notorious, is advocacy of genocide against a racial group. The question is: Must we tolerate advocacy of ideas that we would under no circumstances put into practice? [Chevigny, p. 121].

Chevigny's answer is *yes:* first of all, if a question is worth answering, i.e. not trivial, and if it can be answered, then it *should* be answered. We must come to grips with the irrational. Secondly, such responsibility is a "guarantee of the rationality of the government" (p. 121). The government prejudges nothing as out of the question, not even the most absurd idea.

Swan, however, goes further in telling us, "The worse falsehoods, the damnedest lies, have their origins not in ideas but in pathologies." I find a distinction blurred here. Single madness is unique, surely? and collective madness is otherwise? Surely there is a difference between the widespread, but local, belief, that the old lady across the street is a witch, and the equally widespread belief that all those who do not speak our language or worship our deity, are the enemy? The one *could* be explained away on the basis of individual psychopathology — but I do not excuse it even on that ground — and the other is explainable only as xenophobia, leading, sooner or later, to war. Even the first belief can bring untold suffering to many people; why sweep it under the rug with the emotional bribe of psychopathology?

As for the moment of Hitler's conversion, enough can be said that the origins of Hitler's rise to domination must forever remain obscure — would be now, if Hitler were still alive. The origins of German nationalism and German Judeophobia, however, are open to public scrutiny; so is Wagner's view of the Jews.

With the last sentence of Swan's quotation, however, I find myself solidly in agreement: "This culture at one and the same time told him what he was and what he must do." This, indeed, is my whole point. If you live in a racist culture, you will accept racist books, racist speakers, racist ideas, with the notion that everybody does it, so it must be okay. The works of Mark Twain may be consulted, *passim.*

Swan goes further; he quotes Justice Oliver Wendell Holmes, Jr., dissenting, in *Gitlow* v. *New York* (1925):

> If, in the long run, the beliefs expressed in proletarian dictatorship are destined to be accepted by the dominant forces of the community, the only meaning of free speech is that they should be given their chance and have their way.[27]

This seems to proceed from the original point made by Chevigny, that nothing is to be prejudged as not worth answering, or as too dangerous to answer. But it goes further than that. It suggests that if the people accept a dictatorship, or seem likely to, all the government can do is let the people have their way. Such a giving of ground would violate our Constitution at some point; or there would be a strident call for a new constitutional convention. In any event, political passion, in any country, no matter how well guarded and regulated, can become a *force majeure.*

Substitute for "proletarian dictatorship" any other idea that you abhor — antisemitism, slavery, the abolition of the First Amendment and of the laws and decrees pursuant thereunto, with the consequence suspension of Swan and Peattie from the nearest yardarm — and you feel, do you not, learned colleagues? — a certain qualm: a "chilling effect" in the lower intestine? Did Justice Holmes surmise that in all probability the dictatorship of the proletariat would not come about until long after he had been gathered to his New England forebears? We shall never know; doubtless he shared Lincoln's faith in the wisdom of the people.

Admittedly, "bad tendency" thinking has its fatal defect: whoever is in power may, and frequently does, decry her predecessor's publications as exemplifying a "bad tendency." Examples are beyond enumeration. However, in this country, we know what Holmes did not know, or was too acclimatized to understand; we do know: whenever anyone in this country starts yakking about the dictatorship of the prolctariat, this country marshals all its forces to shut that person up. Similar motions abroad are threatened by forces military, paramilitary, or covert: the First Amendment, and similar guarantees in the constitutions of other countries, to the contrary notwithstanding.

Some librarians are well aware of this challenge, and (like the Data Center in Oakland, California) make available, or occasionally publish, files on governmental suppression of information. For many librarians, long aware of the nature of their communities and their place on the political spectrum, the safe position is a little to the right of center. Our belief in access as a remedy for controversy is girded by the assumption that nothing really disturbing will be said. After all, even the "Free Speech Movement," active on the Berkeley campus of the University of California in 1964, eventually fell silent, broke up, and drifted away.

On the other hand, if the beliefs of the dominant community, even when mistaken or prejudiced, are to sweep all before them in the name of free speech plus majority rule, then it seems useless to stand up for intellectual freedom or even to have an independent judiciary. If we face a mob of bigoted hecklers, then they *are* the townspeople. But neither Holmes, nor Swan, nor I, could survive in such an atmosphere.

The superior weapon which even a few may muster, in the face of bigots and hecklers, is possession of the truth, i.e., the facts. That facts are worth accumulating, let the career of Sanford Berman illustrate. Berman, now of Hennepin County Library, Minnesota, was working in an African library as a catalog librarian when he came across the Library of Congress subject heading: KAFFIRS. Several of his African coworkers told him that this was an Arabic word meaning "unbeliever," a pejorative term applied to their own people. Further investigation showed Berman that LC's *List of subject headings* abounded in pejorative and inaccurate terms, which he identified and exposed in his *Prejudices and antipathies.*[28] He thereby launched a movement, won first resistance, then grudging acceptance; and was finally awarded the American Library Association's Margaret Mann Citation, for distinguished work in cataloging and classification.

The significance of Berman is not that he nudged the Library of Congress into changing subject headings, nor even that nearly all his proposed changes, implemented in his own library first, are obviously justified. He has been criticized for changes made to please a specific group, and with lacking a theoretical basis for his work. But the real significance of Berman is not that of crusader but that of scholar. His critical articles are attended with a barrage of footnotes. Berman has therefore enhanced free speech rather than diminished it, by his criticisms. Instead of distorting the historical record, he has reminded us of what that record really is.

Further, by doing his best to influence library — and therefore public — usage, Berman has enlarged the domain of free speech by widening the territory of free-speakers. For I find nowhere contradicted my thesis that a society which respects the dignity of the individual or the dignity of whole peoples is more free than one which further insults and injures the already insulted and injured, by contesting or denying the real history of their oppression.

To return to Swan: with his point that conformity in ideas, however enforced, renders the intellectual atmosphere stale, I can certainly agree, while pointing out that the corruption of the intellectual atmosphere by racism and pseudoscience renders the atmosphere suffocating, and dangerous. Surely there must be a way by which we can preserve our liberty and our sensitivity too: without appealing to laws and courts, or trying to preserve our patience while debating ideologues and bigots.

Swan correctly points out the futility of the prohibition of "obscene" literature, as an example of the importance of access, and here I take no issue with him at all. I try to deal with the whole "porn mess" in an appendix, and I suspect that I will fare no better with it than the other librarians who have tried to deal with it. On the other hand, while at both Bennington College and the University of California, Davis, there are library materials which some would find offensive, neither of us would go out and buy the contents of an "adult bookstore" to demonstrate our commitment to intellectual freedom. Those who want access to that kind of material in gross can jolly well look elsewhere. Censorship? No, sense, cents, and sensitivity.

Swan's essay "The ethics of freedom" is hard to disagree with in its emphasis on the essential tension within the profession between giving the community what it likes to read and giving it the information that it needs. He is perfectly right in insisting that every thinking librarian ought to be aware of this tension, although he might have noted that the tension is different in an academic library than in a public library, and that the demands of faculty are of a different order and carry more political weight than the demands of a person in tennis shoes. However, I can top his witchcraft story: a librarian friend, married to a career Army officer, endeavored to organize a library in a small Oklahoma town next door to the post to which her husband was assigned. She initially won some supporters, but when it came time to discuss what books should be in the library, the Oklahomans erupted in such bitter wrangling that the library was never opened at all. Captain McInerney was subsequently transferred to West Point, where the library, undoubtedly full of juicy reading, is off-limits to unauthorized personnel, and of course, to the public.

I can top his story of the woman who objected to a communist book in Vermont, too: a friend of mine, a small-press publisher, in his youth wanted to play baseball. Faced with his military service requirement (this was in the fifties), he enlisted in the Air Force, which like the other armed services, has an excellent sports program. The Air Force sent him to the Panama Canal, where A.D., who grew up on the tough streets of San Francisco, knew how to stay out of trouble. While he was there, a company of small-town boys from Minnesota and the Dakotas, country lads just out of basic training, arrived at the base. Once they got leave to visit the neighboring cities of Panama City and Colon, they got into situations that their innocence left them unprepared for. They didn't know what drugs do to your head, and they thought that a friendly girl was just like the girls back home. A number of them became addicted, and others came down with sexually transmitted diseases. Over-protected by their parents, teachers, pastors and (perhaps) librarians, they were on the sick list in a very short time, and of little use to the Air Force or themselves. As for A.D., his only misfortune was to tear a ligament in his leg, an eventuality for which he was perhaps prepared, and which (after some mismanagement on the part of the doctors) finally got him out of the service.

Access, in short, we cherish because it leads to truth, and had the truth been told to these Great Plains men, they might have had a happier career in the service. Their option would have been better directed by a knowledge of the truth. On this, surely, Swan and I can find agreement.

Where we still have disagreement is on the last pages of his essay, where he asks, "Who is to determine which untruths are actually deliberate falsehoods?" The question is a perfectly valid one. He immediately adds, "we all agree that the Holocaust was a genuine, if unspeakably terrible, reality, but 'we' doesn't include everyone. And if 'we' decide by fiat that our truth is never to be assailed by misguided argument, we are not assuring its safety against the outsiders; we are merely converting a perfectly sound truth into an emotional dogma, a distinct step downward in the forum of ideas."

This is a very powerful statement, and his use of the phrase "emotional dogma," is especially telling. There is no question that a number of emotional dogmas circulate in this country. On the left it is heresy *not* to believe that President John F. Kennedy was assassinated as a result of a conspiracy, probably involving some high government officials, likely enough including those of the Central Intelligence Agency, despite the fact that no officials have ever been publicly named (to my knowledge) as having been involved in the assassination, and it passes my poor understanding what good it would do the Central Intelligence Agency to murder the Commander-in-Chief. On the right a similar dark muttering may be heard when the names of Pearl Harbor and Yalta are mentioned. I believe we are now witnessing the belief of a new emotional dogma, that of the deliberate making of the AIDS virus at Fort Detrick, Maryland, for the purpose of eliminating gays, blacks, and drug users from the population. It is still too early to see what damage this rumor-mongering will do to the real, if belated, fight against the virus. If the rumor should turn out to be true, then the people who started it would still be at fault for releasing the information without the responsible sources to back it up. The only article I have seen on this was in an anarchist paper which was remarkably reticent about proof, referring the reader to books by authors I'd never heard of, but eloquent in reasoning by analogy and innuendo. I gave my copy to a friend who maintains a clipping file on the subject. I can't help but wonder about the thoughts of the students who go through the clipping file.

Still there is an enormous difference between conspiracy theories that some people — otherwise sane — hold on to for dear life, the Wilbur Glenn Volivas of our age — and the mountain of information about the Holocaust. Who is to decide the difference? May we not summon a cloud of witnesses? Are not witnesses the principal sources of evidence in our country's courts of law? As for decreeing what is true by fiat, such a thought was never in my mind. Of course, neither the California Library Association nor any other body may define the truth *a priori;* but if the truth is generally known, then deciding to hear someone dispute it will surely require a greater justification than that of simply keeping us properly uncomfortable and undogmatic. We have, after all, other things to do, as librarians, whether skeptic or credulous.

If McCalden had been allowed to speak, if the police had been able to protect the hotel, if no large vases had been overturned and no librarians been frightened out of their wits — what would we have proved? That we are willing, as librarians, to go to every possible length to defend the rights of an unpopular speaker? Or would we have proved that we have little sense of history, and are willing to back the most absurd of causes to prove a point of principle? For I doubt that anyone there was really interested in McCalden's ideas for their own sake, or that he would have made a single convert. If we weren't serious about him, is it not really unfair to McCalden to pretend to take him seriously? Is he not sensitive in his own way?

Swan and I would probably agree that in every society there are emotional dogmas, taboos, unmentionable subjects and persons too sacred to be mentioned without reverence. In Turkey, I understand, there is a law against saying anything bad about Atatürk, although he has been dead for fifty years. In China, although the cultural revolution has been de-capitalized and only placed between quotation marks in the pages of *Beijing review,* the status of Mao Zedong depends on where in China he is mentioned. In the cities he is Comrade Mao, a great military leader who, at the head of the country, made mistakes in his later years. In the country, he is still Chairman Mao, and he made few if any mistakes. The question is, what are our folkways, mores, customs and taboos? We have them: who shapes them? My answer will be, the interaction of the popular mind and the intellectuals, working through and against the media. And all have a responsibility.

VIII.

I must reiterate that John Swan and I have a fairly narrow range of disagreement. If we were to find ourselves on the same intellectual freedom committee, deciding which cases to pursue and which to let go, I suspect we would agree together on about 99 out of 100 cases. Were some latter-day McCarthy (to use one of his own examples) to demand the banning of books from federal libraries, I dare say John and I would stand shoulder-to-shoulder in defense of that most precious of all rights, never enacted, ever to be defended: what Lillian Smith called *the right to be different*. In the few cases where we would disagree, sharply or cautiously, it would be where the speaker, film, or book, defended something that wasn't so, and which would hurt a lot of people if it came to be generally believed that *was* so.

This brings us back to the Big Lie and its implications. I hold that truth is primary to freedom on (at least) some occasions: those in which convention has established a truth — however defined — that the rest of us contemn at our peril. For example, it is the case that we drive on the right side of the road in America, the left side in Britain. Suppose I forget, or ignore, these simple rules of the road; either I am immediately stopped, or I stay home in perplexity, trying to find out which way is which. In either case, I am restricted, I am not free to drive: exactly the case of those who have not read the signs correctly. In the McCalden case, it could be argued, there is a dispute over which way the signs should point; but for me, the point has always been: who switched the signs around? Who made white black, black white, the worse appear the better cause? The question is as old as Socrates, and yet not even Socrates answered it. To this day we punish, however feebly, the people who reverse or destroy trail signs in California's mountains.

IX.

Now let us turn to the activities of those who got a racist Big Lie in their teeth and ran with it — ran with it to the destruction, division, and humiliation of their own country: I mean the Germans, between the two World Wars. Here I will be exploring the roots of antisemitism in the formative years of German nationalism (1870–1945).

Rosenberg and Myers[29] discuss the philosophical underpinnings of the Holocaust; the contributors to their book make plain that the passive acceptance of the pseudoscience of "eugenics" and the gradual absorption of antisemitism by intellectuals made the destruction of the European Jews socially acceptable and therefore physically possible. Out of Germany's sixty millions, Jews constituted only 1 percent. Their disappearance was ignored by many, and their protests met with indifference or contempt.[30]

Baum minimizes the role of antisemitism in German history and emphasizes bureaucratic indifference ("just doing my job") and indifference of the bystanders as the problem. Educated people were involved in genocide; commanders of the *Einsatzgruppen,* platoons that rounded up Jews in newly-occupied towns and executed them, were all university men; 43 percent held the doctorate. For Baum, because of the rise of scientific thinking and bureaucracy, the possibilities for large-scale amoral conduct are deeply woven into the fabric of modern life.[31]

Laurence Thomas's chapter discusses the weakness of liberalism in confronting absolute evil, a weakness displayed in its limited capacity for outrage:

> The ideological foundation on which a society is built profoundly influences the moral sensibilities of its members. The idea of liberalism is harmonious non-interference. And it is this ideal that makes it so easy to rationalize indifference or failing to offer assistance as justified non-interference. As I have characterized it, the liberal conception of society tends to deaden the moral senses.[32]

This will no doubt anger some liberals, for whom the liberal conception of society is the most moral of all; but unless a liberal can get beyond harmonious noninterference, and take a stand on truth as well as freedom, he is likely to be victimized, as Chamberlain was at Munich.

Perhaps the most devastating of these critiques is the one by Martin P. Golding[33] who finds the metaphor of "pathology," applied to the Nazis, insufficient to explain their radically evil actions. Those who accepted the Nazi ideology and values considered themselves "healthy" and therefore right: in killing Jews, they were simply expelling "bad blood" from the German "race." For Eichmann and others, National Socialism was nothing but "applied biology"; Jews were a disease in the body politic which had to be removed for that body to be healthy again. Virchow's theory of "general pathology" saw disease as the degeneration of normal procedures, physiology encountering obstacles. "If Nazi morality was pathological it was because false nonmoral beliefs (e.g. 'racial science') were used in deriving concrete propositions."[34] Laws in Nazi Germany were inverted: old laws repealed and their contraries enacted; consequently Eichmann and his ilk could claim, at the war crimes trials, that everything they were accused of doing was "perfectly legal." Of course: certain activities, previously forbidden, had been made legal so that those activities could be carried out without question.

The general claim of *Echoes from the Holocaust* is that technology + bureaucracy + moral indifference + pseudoscience + antisemitism + obedience = Holocaust. If this is the case then the conclusion which several authors draw—that it could happen again, anywhere, to anybody, and by anybody—does not seem too wildly implausible. Against this argument I must admit that conditions in North America are very different. It is not that Americans and Canadians are free of the sin of racism. It is rather that in Germany and Eastern Europe, as later in Cambodia, Ethiopia, and East Timor, the killers made themselves secure against interference: first by suppressing internal law and destroying social controls, then by closing the frontiers to penetration by potential rescuers.

While it would be paranoid to suggest that a wave of racist terror is about to sweep across America, there have been enough recent conflicts among ethnic groups in American cities, notably Miami, to give the liberal mind uneasiness. Many will say that the answer to speech is more speech, that the answer to racism is to denounce racism, and the answer to McCalden is to have some person, on the platform or in the audience, stand up and tell him off. To my knowledge no one in the program was prepared to do anything of the sort. As for the speech vs. more speech principle: —to be effective, it needs to be carried out sincerely. What distressed many viewers of the American Library Association film, *The speaker,* is that the people (mostly blacks) who insisted on dignity and respect as having priority over free speech, were made to look ridiculous.

To return to our survey of the literature: Pulzer[35] shows how the rise of modern antisemitism in Germany and Austria began with some completely forgotten individuals. While antisemites nowhere succeeded in forming a powerful party of their own before 1914, the economic instability and political insecurities of the two great prewar Central European empires made it possible for the large Conservative parties gradually to take up antisemitism and make it tacitly respectable. Both empires were torn by ethnic conflict, Austria-Hungary especially. The Jew, having no land of his own, became the ultimate "foreign element" held responsible for the two nations' inability to gain economic security and political unity.

Max Weinrich has documented in detail the collaboration of

German scholars in all fields with a rising and ultimately triumphant antisemitic campaign, directed from Nazi headquarters. Even intellectuals, initially opposed to the program, were eventually drawn into the network of the Nazi regime. Those who objected to the racist theories of Alfred Rosenberg and others, based their objections not on the fabrications of these Nazi writers, but to a perception of Nazi beliefs as being "simply vulgar." Institutes and conferences on the "Jewish problem" were set up, with scholars brought in by train or plane from countries under German occupation.[36]

According to Benno Müller-Hill[37] Weinrich's book has never been translated into German. Müller-Hill describes the participation of anthropologists, psychologists, and other social scientists — first in the dismissal of Jews from their collegial positions as well as from the positions occupied by their support staff, and then in the selection of Jews and Gypsies (Romani), both children and adults, for experimentation and extermination. Later, with the destruction of many (but not all) records, a collective amnesia set in, as Müller-Hill tells it:

> After the war, those who returned to university life were, at first, proving to each other that they had known nothing and done nothing.... They never doubted their science.... Almost no one stopped to think that there could be something wrong with psychiatry, with anthropology, or with behavioural science. The international scientific establishment reassured their German colleagues that it had been indeed the unpardonable misconduct of a few individuals, but that it lay outside the scope of science [p. 87].

It is not immediately clear what is "wrong" with the behavioral sciences, but it is at least possible, as "Operation Camelot" in President Arturo Frei's Chile showed, that social scientists can as easily be co-opted into a government plan as physicists or chemists. The point I am making applies to all learned persons, including librarians: intellectuals are not immune from the temptations of racism.

Müller-Hill then addresses himself to "Nine questions":

1. Why was it that the mass murder of Jews, Gypsies, asocial individuals, Slavs, and mental patients took place under German Fascism rather than elsewhere?
2. Where did anti–Semitism come from?

3. What made doctors especially liable to become the apostles of destruction?
4. Why was the extermination of the Jews and of mental patients a secret?
5. Was there a "plan" from the beginning for the extermination of mental patients, the Jews, the Gypsies, and the Slavs?
6. Could National Socialism happen again in Germany or anywhere else?
7. Are the experimental studies of Professors Hallervorden and von Verschuer, mentioned in this book, to be rejected because they constitute "bad science" or were "unscientific," or because they were carried out on appropriate experimental subjects, i.e., on human beings who had been deprived of all their rights?
8. What can we learn about anthropology and psychiatry from the massive experiment of the National Socialist anthropologists and psychiatrists?
9. The last question is whether there were anthropologists or psychiatrists in Germany who did not conform, and who would not fit into the picture I have sketched here.[38]

The answers he gives, as you might anticipate, are comfortless to the optimistic mind. So are the responses to the last question, which are recorded interviews with the elderly scholars and scientists, or with their surviving kinfolk. Scholars and relatives alike, they generally remember only selectively: or not at all.

It could still be argued, and I will concede it, that the answer to pseudoscience is real science, as the answer to lies is "more (i.e. 'true') speech." Unfortunately, the way that intellectuals, and also churchmen, fell into line after Hitler took power, is not reassuring. If only ten scholars had said, to the Nazi racist propaganda, "The whole thing is wrong from beginning to end," would history have changed? Probably not, but W.H. Auden would not have been able to write his line, "Intellectual disgrace/ Stares from every human face" (from *In memory of William Butler Yeats*), if more people, within Germany and without, had protested against what was happening to Germany's ethnic minorities.

At this point, readers, we have touched the nadir of the libertarian conscience. We have discovered that there is no constitution that cannot be rewritten, that no outworn prejudice can be completely eradicated, that no amount of education can resist all social pressures and make its doctors incorruptible. I sugggest that those most likely to style themselves "Incorruptible," like Robespierre, are most likely nearest temptation.

X.

The defense of the libertarian position in freedom of information discussions usually rests on an appeal to the work of John Stuart Mill. In his book *On liberty* (1859), Mill states:

> The object of this essay is to assert one very simple principle, as entitled to govern absolutely the dealings of society with the individual in the way of compulsion and control, whether the means used be of physical force in the form of legal penalties or the moral coercion of public opinion. That principle is that the sole end for which mankind are warranted, individually or collectively, in interfering with the liberty of action of any of their number is self protection. That the only purpose for which power can be rightfully exercised over against any member of a civilized community, against his will, is to prevent harm to others.[39]

Note, first of all, that Mill rules out not only government intimidation but public censure: the disapproving frown, the swish of a crinoline as a back disappears through a door. Note, also, that who the "others" are, is not defined; presumably the "others" are other human beings. In a Millian universe it might be very difficult to get laws enacted to protect wilderness or endangered species; unless the wilderness and wildlife were to be defined as somehow or other the possession of the sovereign. We have come that far from Mill. But let him continue:

> His own good, either physical or moral, is not a sufficient warrant. He cannot rightfully be compelled to do or forbear because it will be better for him to do so, because it will make him happier, because, in the opinions of others, to do so would be wise or even right. These are good reasons for remonstrating with him, or reasoning with him, or persuading him, or entreating him, but not for compelling him or visiting him with any evil in case he do otherwise. To justify that, the conduct from which it is desired to deter him must be calculated to produce evil to someone else. The only

> part of the conduct of anyone for which he is amenable to society is
> that which concerns others. In the part which merely concerns him-
> self, his independence is, of right, absolute. Over himself, over his
> own body and mind, the individual is sovereign [Mill, ch. 1, p. 9].

Note the emphasis on "the moral coercion of public opinion," the
"opinions of others," "remonstrating," "reasoning," "persuading,"
and "entreating," all characteristic of Victorian society with a strong
family kernel, a church surrounded by controversy, a kingdom
stressed by the rise of industrialism. Note, also, the phrase "calculated to produce evil": negligence, then as now a part of English law,
is not taken up here.

Mill did not live in our century of one-party states, of mass
media and totalitarian propaganda. He does, however, show concern with the tyranny of the majority, and the force of unexamined
public opinion (ch. 1, p. 3–9). His idea of public opinion seems
largely concerned with questions of religion and morals; familiar
with a society more homogeneous in race and religion than Britain
is today, he does not concern himself with the stigma of prejudice.
The process of stigmatization, which begins by defining some group
as dangerous to the state and society, and continues by designating
some leader or party as appropriate to resolve the situation, by expelling or annihilating the group deemed unworthy of protection, is
not explicitly covered by Mill.

While Mill, therefore, cannot be faulted for not anticipating
the possibility of a Hitler, those of us who seek his defense of liberty
to construct a defense of our own, should be aware of the limitations
that his period in history places on him. The problem closest to ours
that Mill does address, the propagation of an opinion some people
dislike, he addresses in the following words:

> . . . the peculiar evil of silencing the expression of an opinion is that
> it is robbing the human race, posterity as well as the existing genera-
> tion — those who dissent from the opinion, still more than those who
> hold it. If the opinion is right, they are deprived of the opportunity
> of exchanging error for truth; if wrong, they lose, what is almost
> as great a benefit, the clearer perception and livelier impression of
> truth produced by its collision with error.[40]

It could be argued that where a racist speaker offers to address
a group in a public forum such as a scholarly association, that truth

will be better served by providing the program with an antiracist speaker to rebut his charges and disprove his alleged "facts"; and on my interpretation of Mill, this would provide a "clearer perception and livelier impression of truth." Such a program, therefore, ought to please Mill and the Millians no end. Aside from the fact that (so far as I know) no such speaker was provided for at the California Library Association conference, the question may be raised, how often are we seriously required to take up settled facts, as apart from opinions? For some readers, the answer will be, every time the truth is challenged, it is necessary to rise to its defense. For others, the answer is that answering racists is not worth it: don't play around with them, don't give them any more platforms than the law allows, or that the rest of us can help.

Mill (who, it is necessary to remind us, is working with his understanding of law and history, not Swan's or Peattie's or any late twentieth-century reader's) deals with the problem in his own way, by examining the argument of the paternalist. While persons and governments are often mistaken, there are some convictions that are right, and because error has befallen human societies before, that does not mean that we are paralyzed and rendered inactive today. Mill sums this view up and answers it:

> Men and governments act to the best of their ability. There is no such thing as absolute certainty, but there is assurance sufficient for the purposes of human life. We may, and must, assume our position to be true for the guidance of our own conduct; and it is assuming no more when we forbid bad men to pervert society by the propagation of opinions which we regard as false and pernicious.
>
> I answer, that it is assuming very much more. There is the greatest difference in assuming an opinion to be true because, with every opportunity for contesting it, it has not been refuted, and assuming its truth for the purpose of not permitting its refutation. Complete liberty of contradicting and disputing our opinion is the very condition which justifies us in assuming its truth for purposes of action; and on no other terms can a being with human faculties have any rational assurance of being right [Mill, ch. 2, p. 18].

How does this apply to the handling of controversy at the conference of the California Library Association? Were those who protested McCalden's appearance among those who presumed the received history of the Holocaust "to be true because, with every opportunity for contesting it, it has not been refuted," or were they among those guilty of "assuming its truth for the purpose of not permitting its refutation?" And is an account of history, as recent and well-attested as that, to be classed as an "opinion"? The same questions, obviously, may be raised about the American Library Association film, *The speaker.* What does "every opportunity for contesting" the traditional views of Jewish history, or of Afro-American intelligence, *mean* — in terms of time, testimony, scientific investigation and publication, reception, scholarly debate and consensus?

Whenever I visualize Mill and his contemporaries in their own time I think of frock-coated gentlemen, in Parliament or common room, discussing, in perfect liberty, "questions": the Eastern Question, the Schleswig-Holstein Question, the Irish Question (the last, still with us). Mill's second chapter, "Of the liberty of thought and discussion," gives example after example of the need for freedom of discussion and of the uninhibited expression of opinion on a wide variety of subjects: "subjects infinitely more complicated, to morals, religion, politics, social relations, and the business of life" (p. 42). Absent from this list of *disputanda* are established scientific and historical *facts.* In the previous sentence he alludes to the dispute between the Copernican vs. the Ptolemaic theory, phlogiston vs. oxygen; but he nowhere suggests that the older model is just as competent to explain observations as the newer, nor would anyone assert that now. Nor does he suggest that the actuality of history may remain in dispute, while the survivors are still around, to put the weight of their testimony in the scale. Consider, then, what Mill would have said to a patriotic but misguided Frenchman who informed him: "Sir, the battle of Waterloo never took place, and anyway, we won it." Surely, Mill would have replied, "Monsieur, you have perfect liberty to speak as you please, but I think those Chelsea pensioners over there know more about the matter than you do."

At what point, finally, may we close our books and say, that while historians may differ in their judgments of leaders, peoples, and events, some things are settled: that the Jews suffered by the millions, that skin is no determinant of educability, that the Schleswig-Holstein Question was settled by the plebiscite of 1920, and that this Earth on which we stand, and into which we will soon enough disappear, is *not* flat, but a spheroid oblate by one part in 297? "Only when boredom with cranks is pandemic," wrote one of my critics in answer to the question above, "every generation suffers this problem." Before I call for a pandemic of boredom — which might easily get out of hand — let Mill answer:

> As mankind improve, the number of doctrines which are no longer disputed or doubted will constantly be on the increase; and the well-being of mankind may almost be measured by the number and gravity of the truths which have reached the point of being un-contested [ch. 2, p. 42].

This leads one to the famous "Millian paradox," cited by many writers on Mill: that as more and more doctrines become solidly established, diversity of opinion will be less and less evident, and the world will be a more united — but more boring — place than it is now. Fortunately the paradox shows no sign of reification. Questions such as abortion, creationism, gun control, the Middle East, Northern Ireland, and welfare reform continue to excite the populace. And well they should! I only express the hope I cannot enforce: that all parties be in possession of the facts, and be honest about expressing them.

I am, incidentally, uncomfortable with Mill's use of the word "doctrines": for me a doctrine is the utterance of a particular party or church, and stands on a different footing than the statement of a witness under oath, or the report of a repeatable (falsifiable, in Popper's use of the term) experiment. To distinguish these two by examples, deliberately chosen for their controversial nature: the literal interpretation of the Bible, i.e., inerrancy, is (in some churches) a doctrine; the great age of the Earth (in terms of billions of years) is demonstrably true.

To refute Mill is as much beyond my powers as it is hostile to my object. After all, a writer who has no use for Mill at all would not (if rational) agree to a debate. My problem with Mill is that, given his assumptions about the audience he is writing for, he does not explicitly state that though opinions may differ, the holders of them should be in possession of the facts, have "done their home-work," in the phrase of the 1960's — and also be honest and sane: neither deceptive nor obsessed with private fantasies.

I introduce here, as a supplement to Mill's thinking, the concept of the "hidden agenda." The person who denies the reality of a historical fact so well established, or a scientific theory so well supported by evidence as the events of 1933–45 or the great age of the Earth, is probably concealing an agenda: the resumption of oppression of the Jews, or the control of public schools by religious fundamentalists.[41]

The reader will ask how I can prove this. Of course, I concede that it is impossible to read anyone's motives; but some evidence is circumstantial. If McCalden is purely disinterested, why did he come to the succeeding California Library Association conference (Long Beach, November 1985), hire a room in the same hotel that the CLA was using as its headquarters, and give a public lecture on the need to protect from deportation persons in this country suspected of having killed Jews in Eastern Europe during the war? If the creationists are purely concerned with the public dissemination of their brand of information, why are they using lawsuits and legislation to insist that teachers in schools give equal time to "creation science"? The vigor with which these efforts have been carried out in recent years does not suggest that the creationists are disinterestedly concerned with the freedom of the marketplace of ideas.[42]

Let me not be guilty of the same arrogance. New views do supersede old. Within the last twenty years the accepted view of the origin of the Earth's continents and islands has been completely revised by the adoption of the plate-tectonics theory, originally proposed as the theory of continental drift by the German scientist Alfred Lothar Wegener (1880–1930). For many years Wegener was regarded as an eccentric, barely tolerated by the majority of the world's geologists. Later evidence, gathered since the Second World War, suggested that a theory or model similar to his described observed facts more completely, and was more comprehensive in resolving their connections; so, views which (without Wegener) might never have been entertained are now the geology of the day.

However, Wegener (and his successors) had no "hidden agenda." They were not out to prove the superiority of any people, the right of any group to any territory, the superiority of any language. No country, church, or party gained, or could gain, from the triumph of plate-tectonics. These geologists in controversy were honest: on whichever side they took their stand, they called the shots as they saw them, without the benefit of lawsuits and special-interest legislation. They revised geology: but they were not "revisionists," with a complaint against a hostile establishment, or a special group to protect or attack. They played fair, they had virtue.

The case for Mill is one so easily espoused, and so frequently, by intellectuals in our society, that it would be almost parricide to attack him: nor do I do so. But just as the United States Constitution has been frequently amended but not supplanted (but we know there are people out there who want to do this: ill-luck befall them!), Mill's immortal paper needs not refutation, but supplementation, in the form of critiques and free discussion. With some of these, at greater or lesser length, I propose to deal.

XI.

Thomas Scanlon, a champion in Mill's field, makes the point[43] that freedom of expression names a group of protected acts (of speech, writing, etc.) which are immune from restriction, although in some cases harm which is normally legislated against might come from such expression. He attempts to show that this situation is not so illogical or irrational as at first it might appear.

For Scanlon, it is difficult to define the class of acts which are protected by this doctrine. Simply saying that whether to justify some acts for their own sake is *not* the question, and that the only real justification for prohibiting certain speech acts is the old "time, place, and manner" rule, — is, for Scanlon, not at all satisfactory. Scanlon does recognize that some acts of expression can indeed cause damage: as when the sound of a voice triggers an avalanche. Assault (threatening with a gun, for example) may be another act of expression to be prohibited. (I would certainly prohibit it, and add that threatening whole classes of people does not enter into his discussion, any more than it enters into Mill's.)

Scanlon then states what he calls the Millian Principle, which he derives from chapter 2 of *On liberty*. (Obviously this is Scanlon's distillation, not a quote from Mill in any sense, direct or indirect):

> There are certain harms which, although they would not occur but for certain acts of expression, nonetheless cannot be taken as part of a justification for legal restrictions on those acts. These harms are: (a) harms to certain individuals which consist in their coming to have false beliefs as a result of those acts of expression; (b) harmful consequences of acts performed as a result of those acts of expression, where the connection between the acts of expression and the subsequent harmful acts consists merely in the fact that the act

of expression led the agents to believe (or increased their tendency to believe) those acts to be worth performing [Scanlon, p. 213].

While not sufficiently comprehensive, the Millian Principle ("MP" hereafter) shows why at least some consequences of the freedom of expression cannot be appealed to as a justification for the application of legal resources against them. The MP rests on the position of the autonomous citizen, vis-a-vis the government: "The harm of coming to have false beliefs is not one that an autonomous man could allow the state to protect him against through freedom of expression" (Scanlon, p. 217). Also, "what must be argued against is the view that the state, once it has declared certain conduct to be illegal, may when necessary move to prevent that conduct by out-lawing its advocacy" (p. 218). Again, "It is important to see that the argument for the Millian Principle rests on a limitation of the authority of states to command their subjects rather than on a right of individuals" (p. 221).

Scanlon himself sees difficulties with the MP: on the basis of this principle citizens could not raise any objection against a government that banned parades of antigovernment protestors, solely with the excuse that parades and demonstrations blocked traffic. The MP needs to be supplemented by other considerations: trade-offs and balances; equitable access to means of expression; the necessary exercise of general political rights, such as freedom of assembly. He also discusses possible wartime and other exceptional circumstances.

In looking at the MP, however, I can spot some other exceptions to it. We all want to be protected from mail fraud and deceptive advertising, and there are laws against such acts of expression. Libel, blackmail, the pyramid letter which asks for money, are all prohibited by law. So is incitement to riot (as for example, lynching), which surely comes under Scanlon's "(b), harmful consequences. . . ." Nobody thinks of such laws as any kind of censorship. The debate over pornography, which ranges feminists who wish to prohibit pornography against others who perceive a greater danger in censoring such material, also revolves around the application of Scanlon's "(b)": if pornography is the theory and rape is the practice, then some women, at least, have a sharp disagreement with Scanlon.

The Millian Principle, then, is a good summary of Mill's thought, but like some other features of Mill, it needs to be re-examined in the light of history. Take the creationists' demand for equal time: on the MP it would be impossible to refuse them their demand for equal time in the schools. In fact, under Scanlon's sentence "(a), harms to certain individuals...," they would gain a distinct advantage; for what's the harm in using for teaching purposes a Book which is alleged by some to be infallible and which, by precept and historical account, teaches boys and girls to be good? Indeed, the creationists' case against evolution includes the statement that it lures young people into wicked ways. (First they start disbelieving in the inerrancy of the Bible, then they stop going to church, then they ... and so on.)

Another problem I find with the MP is that it provides no check against falsehoods uttered by government officials. These have been so numerous recently, and the cloak of presidential prerogative and legislative immunity so frequently thrown around them, that it would be tedious to mention each one in detail. The problem is that in most cases, the official resigns or retires, no judicial action is taken (or is impossible), and the weary people can only look around for new leaders to help them out of the mess.

Of course I am not suggesting that we prosecute a member of Congress who supports an unpopular and unsuccessful war; that would bring confusion to government, and the Constitution specifically prohibits such prosecution.[44] However, considering that most members of Congress are returned to office even after several terms, that incumbents have a definite financial advantage over challengers, the time-honored method of "voting the rascals out" is no longer as effective as formerly.

If we apply the Millian Principle to libraries, of course, we are on much safer ground. No librarian will ban a murder mystery because someone might decide to use the writer's favorite weapon on a real person; and as for government officials, they may be freely questioned by an audience of librarians whenever they choose to address such an audience. In my experience, government officials usually turn up at library conferences just after they have done something good for libraries. The question whether a racist should address a library conference, then, comes under a different heading than the Millian Principle. Since librarians are not to be moved to commit illegal acts just by hearing a racist, the question is not of freedom of information or of access, but of personal and collective self-respect.

The most thorough criticism I have yet seen of Mill is that provided by Frederick Schauer, lawyer turned philosopher, who begins his *Free speech* by taking his stand on principles: "Principles," he tells us, "are the currency of political philosophy."[45] By *principle* he means an independent principle: such a principle may be an instance of a broader principle, but if it is independent it covers a wide variety of causes and reasons. Independence is relative: in this case we mean that a principle is independent relative to other, equally sovereign, principles.

Free speech, for Schauer, is such an independent principle. We do not talk about it in connection with other forms of liberty, but prefer to treat it by itself. True, the First Amendment does link it with other freedoms and consequent restrictions on government. But this is because the First Amendment is not a code of laws, but an "omnibus bill" (Schauer, p. 3).

The implication of this "omnibus bill" philosophy is that, when government must suppress free speech to reach a goal, the justification for that suppression of free speech must be greater than it would be if other liberties are suppressed (e.g., the right of *habeas corpus*). The Free Speech Principle demands a special consideration among other principles: when principles are to be sacrificed, Free Speech gets first choice among the lifeboats. This does not mean that *no* speech may *ever* be restricted. "A Free Speech Principle implies only that restrictions on speech require *some* greater justification" (Schauer, p. 9).

For Schauer, speech is an other-regarding act:

> ...speech clearly can and frequently does cause harm. These harms include harms to the speaker, harm to society, and harm to the governing apparatus of the state.... These are examples of comparatively immediate effects of speech. There can be longer-term effects as well. What people say or publish may influence widely-held views about politics or morality.... Even "abstract" discussion can have similar effects [Schauer, p. 10].

Schauer continues:

> Mill treats speech as a member of the other category [other-regarding acts]. Under neither of these interpretations is there any suggestion that speech is ineffectual, or that it is incapable of causing unpleasant consequences.
>
> If there is a Free Speech Principle, it protects certain conduct not because it is self-regarding, but *despite* the fact that it is other-regarding.

If I understand Schauer correctly, and if he is interpreting Mill correctly, the Free Speech Principle does not just protect the individual speaker, but protects him or her in relation to his audience. Seen thus, "speech" covers a multitude of activities: hiring someone to do a murder is a "speech act"; so, for free speech purposes, is wearing a black armband in protest against a war. The Free Speech Principle may turn out to be not one but a cluster of principles.

Schauer next defines what he calls the "argument from truth":

> Throughout the ages many diverse arguments have been employed to attempt to justify a principle of free speech. Of all these, the predominant and most persevering has been the argument that free speech is particularly valuable because it leads to the discovery of truth. Open discussion, free exchange of ideas, freedom of enquiry, and freedom to criticize, so the argument goes, are necessary conditions for the effective functioning of the process of searching for truth [Schauer, p. 15].

This theory Schauer characterizes as the marketplace of ideas, which I have discussed before. Schauer finds fault with this theory for reasons different from either Swan's or mine. For Schauer, central to this free marketplace is an *adversary:* confronted with this adversary, an "invisible hand," like the one invoked by Adam Smith, will insure that the best ideas emerge. The validity of the argument turns on the legitimacy of its goal: it assumes that truth is valuable, which Schauer is willing to grant. Truth is not defined theoretically, since this argument cuts across all theories of truth. Nor is it inconsistent with scepticism: we may uphold the argument even if we are not 100 percent sure of what particular truth we have found.

For Schauer, this lack of a definition of truth is a weakness in the "argument from truth." If we have an argument that purports to lead us to the truth, without being able to evaluate the truth we have in hand, then our argument or method of going about the truth is weak. "This view of truth appears to collapse any distinction between fact and value, between factual statements and normative statements." (p. 18).

This objection does not strike me as entirely valid. By a process of inquiry, Swan's half-truths and "untruths" might be, under ideal conditions, stripped away, so that what remained, "however improbable," in Sherlock Holmes's phrase, would be the truth. I suggest that this is what Swan and some others would like to see; and had we but world enough and time, it might happen. However, let Schauer continue:

> Stipulating that increased knowledge is a valuable end does not help to answer the central question — does granting a special liberty of discussion and communication aid us in reaching that end? Is the marketplace of ideas more likely to lead to knowledge than to error, ignorance, folly, or nonsense?
>
> To many people this question answers itself. They assert that free and open discussion of ideas is the only rational way of achieving knowledge, and they assume that the mere assertion of this proposition is proof of its truth. This is of course unsatisfactory. Without a causal link between free speech and knowledge the argument from truth must fail [Schauer, p. 19].

Schauer's second paragraph seems a stronger argument. Marketplaces are notoriously noisy, jostling, crowded places with little time to examine each fruit for soft spots, each horse for wrung withers. Indeed, if the marketplace of ideas includes the nonideas and disinformation now spread by the media, including television, we may well despair of ever getting clear of "error, ignorance, folly, or nonsense."[46] One way to avoid this dilemma is to define truth in terms of the process of discussion: whatever is accepted after discussion is good, what is rejected is false, or bad; and any decision imposed by fiat, however well-intended, must have something wrong with it *ipso facto*. It's the process that matters: truth is the result of a process, merges with, becomes part of, that process, and "to travel hopefully is better than to arrive." Schauer sees serious weaknesses in this line of argument. Rational discussion is not more necessarily valuable than decision by executive order; and the freedom-of-discussion argument assumes, *a priori,* that open inquiry is preferable as a matter of course. In other countries, truth is settled by dictators, politburos, or ayatollahs; the fact that in the Anglo-American universe of discourse we prefer open discussion displays our own cultural traditions.

I find this not as strong an argument: we are, after all, discussing intellectual freedom in an American context, not in the context of those countries where, to borrow a phrase from Lincoln, "they make no pretense of liberty." However, Schauer sees the marketplace of ideas as leading to the triumph not of truth but of consensus, and for Schauer, consensus theory leads to extreme sub-jectivism: if there is free and open discussion, then whatever the prevailing view is, it is the right one, certainly in an open society such as ours. We would have to say (Schauer tells us) that American for-eign policy, despite all its turns and twists, was basically right at all times in the past thirty years, since there has been virtually unlimited freedom of discussion in the United States during that time.

Schauer assumes in this statement, however, that foreign policy is dictated by public opinion. During the past thirty years the con-trary sometimes has been true; and only after long effort has public opinion then been able to surmount the effective propaganda cam-paign of the government and its allies. Public opinion, in short, is indeed that "compound of desirability and appearance" that Swan quotes Ambrose Bierce as characterizing truth. The marketplace of ideas contains much junk; and lacking a market police, such as we would find in a bazaar, or even a Securities and Exchange Commis-sion of ideas (Heaven forfend!), we are ultimately left to our own devices in deciding what is true.

What about the theory that says that allowing contrary opin-ions to be expressed is the best way that we can test them and thus arrive at the facts? For Schauer, this assumes that the suppression of an opinion is based solely on the perceived falsity of that opinion. That is not necessarily so. It may be that truth lies in the suppressed opinion. "If this is so, then a general policy of prohibiting the ex-pression of opinions thought to be false extinguishes *some* knowl-edge and perpetuates *some* error" (p. 24). Schauer here seems to be talking about Swan's half-truths or truths that still need qualifica-tion, addition, or amendment (e.g., "The United States is responsi-ble for the Cold War"; the statement surely needs *partly* inserted into it). The protection, therefore, given to the expression of con-trary or false opinions, is not given so that we may test them and discard them, but is given lest we discard them too hastily and thereby lose the hidden partial truths that they might contain.

For Schauer, both suppression of speech and freedom of speech involve a large degree of uncertainty:

> Therefore we are merely guessing when we suppress; but we are also guessing when we decide not to suppress. If the expression of an opinion possibly causes harm, allowing that opinion expression in-volves some possibility of harm. If the suppression of that opinion entails the possible suppression of truth, then suppression also

entails some probability of harm. Suppression is necessarily wrong only if the former harm is ignored. Therefore a rule absolutely prohibiting suppression is justified only if speech can never cause harm, or if the search for truth is elevated to a position over all other values [Schauer, p. 29].

For librarians, this dark passage has at least one possible implication: they can't have it both ways. If speech can never cause harm, then obviously the suppression of books is not only bad, it is useless, misdirected: "No girl was ever seduced by a book." The antipornography feminists, however, think at least some men have been corrupted by them; but let us leave them to one side for a moment. If no one is corrupted by books, then it seems likely that no one is greatly improved by them, either; in which case the Young Adult reviewers are wasting their time. Perhaps this misgiving about our emphasis on books and reading lies at the heart of the profession: perhaps this is why the posters for sale at American Library Association conferences command: "READ!" with an illustration of a popular film star or a character reading in unqualified obedience. Of course there are many other things to do with one's time besides read; and shorn of any grammatical object (read *what?*), the injunction loses its force and becomes simply an invitation to kill time.

As to the rest of Schauer's "suppression" passage above, it seems to me difficult enough. Schauer seems to be saying that we are in the dark when we decide either to suppress speech or to permit it; and yet he does not take a completely libertarian position ("a rule absolutely prohibiting suppression is justified only if speech can never cause harm" which of course is not the case). I do not know what he means, finally, when he says "if the search for truth is elevated to a position over all other values." I only mention it to distance myself from it: I posit not that truth or the search for truth takes priority over all other values; otherwise I would be a Platonist, banishing all poets from my Republic. I only posit that some knowledge of the truth, and some commitment to living in its light, are necessary conditions for the exercise of professional life and intellectual freedom.

Schauer next turns to the argument from democracy, which he finds confined to a narrow range of societies. Recognizing that "democracy" as a word has been distorted almost hopelessly by propaganda, he applies the word in its strictest sense to mean

> a system that acknowledges that ultimate political power resides in
> the population at large, that the people as a body are sovereign, and
> that they, either directly or through their elected representatives, ac-
> tually control the operation of government [Schauer, p. 36].

Schauer associates the argument from democracy most closely with
the name of Alexander Meiklejohn, who (according to Schauer,
p. 39) "saw all democracies as New England town meetings writ
large." Under this simplification of the political life of the larger
republic, two critical elements support the Free Speech Principle: all
relevant information must be made available to the electorate in
order that they may vote intelligently; and the people as a whole being sovereign, government officials must be servants rather than
rulers. It follows that censorship by government is anomalous, since
the servants would, by censoring information, restrict the ability of
the sovereign to govern. And finally the role of government as ser-
vant allows the people as sovereign to criticize, reject, even impeach
its servants as leaders.

Governments not being able, or not being allowed, to decide
for the people what is true and what is false, only the people as
sovereign can make that decision. The drawback to this argument
may be recollected by every adult who was told on the playgrounds
of childhood, "You're outvoted!" Applied to adult life, and in the
sphere of intellectual freedom, authority (and the power to delegate
authority) can actually work to the detriment of free speech.

> If the people may entrust Jones with the exclusive obligation and
> authority to round up stray dogs, why may it not entrust Brown
> with the exclusive authority to determine truth or falsity, or to exer-
> cise a power of censorship over publications? [Schauer, p. 40].

There are those who think the village librarian has just that
authority: some wish she would stop, some wish she would do it
more. The *Newsletter* of the Freedom to Read Foundation may be
consulted, *passim*. But to return to Schauer: the Free Speech Principle, which started out as a brake on sovereign authority, has now
lost its effectiveness; free speech becomes a mere platitude, and
"You're outvoted!" shouts down truth itself. Readers of Henrik
Ibsen's play, *An enemy of the people,* will recall the way in which
a town meeting is turned against the teller of an unpleasant truth.
Schauer avoids the ultimate indignity wrought upon the minority by

the majority — withdrawal of the right of suffrage — and looks to the idea of equality as a corrective to the tyranny of the majority. But this corrective only is possible if the majority is already committed to equality (in which case the tyranny of the majority would never arise).

> As we shift from a sterile notion of democracy as majority rule to democracy as equal participation, free access becomes more a matter of individual dignity, individual choice, and equal treatment of all individuals, and less an idea grounded in notions of sovereignty [Schauer, p. 41].

The school playground phrase, "You're outvoted!" would be replaced by "It's her turn now" or "Let's give everyone a chance."

Schauer also approaches the "slippery-slope" argument, usually given as the query, "Where do we stop?" If we suppress one idea, so the logic goes, all expression is in danger. Librarians often invoke the slippery-slope argument when defending a book they themselves do not like. *They* wouldn't have wasted money on the worthless title, but a librarian in the next county bought it; and so *aux armes, citoyens,* let us rush to the defense of the odious tome: it's the principle, don't you know.

Schauer seems more impressed with the slippery-slope argument than I am. He quotes Lord Chesterfield, speaking against the Theatres Act of 1737:

> There is such a connection between licentiousness and Liberty, that it is not easy to correct the one, without dangerously wounding the other. It is extremely hard to distinguish the true limit between them; like a changeable silk, we can easily see that there are two different colors, but we cannot easily discover where the one ends, or the other begins [Schauer, p. 83].

An excellent argument against the antipornography statutes. Whether Lord Chesterfield always made the distinction between licentiousness and Liberty in his own life, let us not inquire. The problem to my mind is to establish that speech is more slippery, more prone to erosion, than other activities. Since it is not quantifiable, it is not like a speed limit, which can be enforced; and yet it is not entirely a private matter, like how long one lets one's hair grow. We all recognize taboos on everyday speech; the laws of libel constrain me from saying certain things about my antagonists. Self-censorship, induced by social pressure, is common to all societies; but the slippery-slope argument is not therefore necessarily to be invoked. We all know that there is a four-letter word for the fellow who says the first thing that comes into his head, and then cries "censorship!" when rebuked; and that word is spelled f-o-o-l.

It is true that if this book is banned in Maine, it might be banned in California: but not necessarily. To suppose that all books, or even the whole collection, is in danger, wherever censors might strike, no matter how far away, is to convert a possibility into a probability and then by gradual degrees to convert that probability into a certainty: a logical fallacy which will convince no one, not even our best friends.

XII.

Schauer's critique of Mill is not a radical dismantling of his thought but rather an updating, an amendment to Mill and those who abide by Millian Principles. The name of Herbert Marcuse is associated with a more radical and political approach to Mill, to the extent that the book *A critique of pure tolerance* is cited as his work, even though he only wrote a third of it.[47]

The first of the three authors, Robert Paul Wolff, criticizes tolerance and pluralism from the point of view of the weakness of government in a pluralist society: the public can only vote for candidates it does not know, on information largely lacking, and government is reduced to bargaining among competing powers with different bases. The second author, Barrington Moore, Jr., puts his reliance on the scientific method, refusing any appeal to religious or purely ethical concerns. Neither thinker gives us a clear idea of what a better society would look like, nor what defects there are in the scientific approach that might prevent the creation of the society desired.

Marcuse's essay, "Repressive tolerance," has completely overshadowed the other two essays, and since Marcuse is so well known to most readers, it seems best to recapitulate his thinking briefly. Marcuse sees the government, plus the media and technology, as constituting a massive conspiracy to mislead and confuse the people. Tolerance is nowadays extended to power as well as to protest, to the right as well as the left, "to movements of aggression as well as to movements of peace, to the party of hate as well as to that of humanity."[48] For Marcuse, this toleration of wrong ideas is intolerable, and the remedy is to de-indoctrinate the public by "information slanted in the opposite direction" (*A critique,* p. 99).

If democracy is blocked, unblocking it, for Marcuse, may require

> apparently undemocratic means. They would include the withdrawal of toleration of speech and assembly from groups and movements which promote aggressive policies, armament, chauvinism, discrimination on the grounds of race and religion, or which oppose the extension of public services, social security, medical care, etc. [Marcuse, *A critique,* p. 100].

This, obviously, may well have been the philosophy of those who threatened to invade, or blockade, the hotel where McCalden was to have appeared on a platform. As I write this, a rally of neo–Nazis and Skinheads is being held in the next county, and an appeal was posted on the University of California's Davis campus to Jews and others to go down to the ranch where it is being held to stage a counter-demonstration. Helicopters, presumably from sheriff's offices, are passing through the rain clouds above my house. Marcuse — and his enemies — do not sleep. Let us only hope that the rain slows the activities of both.

I cite Marcuse only to distance myself from him. Disruption only leads to further disruption, and eventually to a war in which all voice of reason or compassion is drummed down. The application to library practice seems to be this, in my view: there seems no need for deliberate offense of a community, nor any need for surprise when the community protests. The case of Salman Rushdie's book, *The satanic verses,* illustrates the point still further.

Rushdie, who holds an M.A. (honours) in history from Cambridge University, wrote a novel widely understood as being insulting to the Prophet Mohammed, with the result that the book was banned in Saudi Arabia, Pakistan, and Iran, and the Ayatollah Khomeini announced a multimillion-dollar reward for anyone who would murder him. Appalled by this last act, writers in New York held a public meeting in which they denounced the Ayatollah and read aloud passages from the book. While nobody thinks that the Ayatollah was right, might I not ask if Rushdie, a former Muslim, was not decidedly foolhardy? And was reading the book aloud at a public meeting in New York just a forthright defense of intellectual freedom? Muslims would say it added insult to injury.[49]

There is, however, some value to Marcuse's point of view: he does perceive that the society we live in is not value-neutral, but is colored by the ideology of the dominant race, gender, and class. He can indeed see that neutrality, objectivity, tolerance, are often used as a cover for the acceptance of racism. It would not be possible to claim that this was the case with the California Library Association; certainly Stefan B. Moses and Bernard Kreissman were not guilty of racism. What the incident reveals, however, as a Marcusean might point out, is that liberal librarians are so conditioned by the responses they have learned in their professional training that they have no way of telling McCalden to "buzz off" without seeming to betray their deepest principles and divide the Association to the sound of anguished recriminations. Because the librarians' rhetoric is not grounded in political reality, their response is divided and inadequate.

John Swan himself anticipates some of these criticisms in his essay, "Librarianship is censorship."[50] Swan points out that the librarian inevitably screens out some material in his acquisition process, on the basis of cost, local interest, etc.; a small library purchases *World book* and lets the local university, if there is one, get the *Great Soviet encyclopedia* in English translation. A certain slant on the world is thereby denied to the small community. For Swan, this is entirely understandable, if not entirely commendable; professional life is full of such compromises, and the battle against censorship must be waged by a librarian who is himself a censor. The whole essay—with which, by the way, I have no quarrel—breathes the understanding of basic tensions between theory and practice in the profession that are demonstrated in his later writings.

So far, I have examined a number of defenses of intellectual freedom: the free marketplace of ideas, the view that truth *is* our freedom, the notion that liberalism is harmonious noninterference, plus such attacks on traditional defenses as those leveled by Handlin, Arendt, Schauer, Wolff, Moore and Marcuse. Mill and his defender Scanlon have also been reviewed. I approach the last defense of all librarians last of all: neutrality.

Neutrality, as applied to librarianship, rests on the time-honored principle that librarians on duty, and libraries functioning, base their credibility on avoiding taking sides. Libraries and librarians best protect their freedom, and justify their use of it, by avoiding partisan political activity, by giving equal time and space to groups in conflict, and offering space in their meeting rooms to locals of whatever political persuasion. This defense of intellectual freedom is as much an exhibition of freedom as a defense of it. The library is neither Democratic nor Republican, but presents information to all, regardless of their politics or persuasions.

This neutrality is so widely accepted, and so embedded in daily professional practice, as well as in the *Library Bill of Rights,* that it might seem a waste of time discussing it. However, it might be interesting to place this principle in the wider context of American and intellectual neutrality.

Till about the 1890s Americans stayed away from the ideological controversies of Europe, while maintaining a loose hegemony over the countries of Latin America, and a tighter rein on Afro-American and Amerindian peoples within its own borders. Women, also, were denied the vote until well into the twentieth century. Few intellectuals came here from Europe for anything more than a short tour of inspection, until the 1920s, and certainly since (post–Civil War) Reconstruction days, most of our intellectuals have been "above the battle" in American politics. Exceptions come to mind, of course; the antislavery movement, the 1930s, the 1960s. As for librarians, although they no longer promote "morally uplifting literature," they have, for the most part, remained *neutral* in political disputes in America.

There was a time, however, when American libraries, and the freedoms they enjoy, were literally consumed in the flames of battle. I refer to the most spectacular event in American library history: the burning on August 24, 1814, of the House of Representatives and the attached Library of Congress, by troops under the command of British General Robert Ross and Admiral (later Sir) George Cockburn. It may or may not be true, as Nye and Morpurgo insist, that Cockburn sat down in the Speaker's chair in the House, and asked his troops, "Shall this harbour of Yankee democracy be burned? All for it will say Aye!"[51] Captain James Pack, R.N., in his biography of Cockburn, omits this detail and briefly gives a kindlier picture of an officer merely carrying out a painful duty.[52]

The point of digging up this ancient atrocity — and by the way, I'll give you three guesses as to where the 83 volumes of Cockburn's manuscripts, including those of his service life, are stored — is not to arouse old indignations, but to point out that, alike for Jefferson (who restored the Library) and Cockburn, the idea of a library open to the public (as aside from private libraries, such as any eighteenth-century gentleman well might have had), is a *political* concept, and democracy, including equal access to information, a *revolutionary* concept, welcome or dreaded, as the case might be.

I can just hear some eighteenth-century conservative splutter: "What, furnish Information upon the Workings of Government to the Labouring Classes? Why, next they will be demanding that Share in the Government, which is properly reserved for their Betters!" Voices like that one are not wanting even today. The demand to remove books, and to block sources of information, is at bottom a Toryish one, whether it comes from the local citizenry, or from the United States Office of Management and Budget. It is often said that libraries today are under fire from the left as well as from the right. I am not so sure of this: most of the protests which some identify as being made by leftwing forces are from people of color who object to books for children and adults which they perceive as racist. The fact that a parent objects to *Little black Sambo* does not tell the librarian whether the parent votes Democratic, Republican, or indeed if she bothers to vote at all. She is concerned with the dignity of her race, not political alignment; and to think of her as "left" is to equate antiracism with socialism: a cardinal error. More importantly, many librarians do not realize that a library is an inherently empowering and liberating institution, as long as it is not subject to censorship.

The libertarian philosophy of librarianship, which gives access to a wide spectrum of information on all subjects, necessarily must include information upon the workings of government which the government may well feel embarrassed to have people know about. Any well-stocked public or academic library in this country should carry, for example, not only books critical of United States policy in Central America, but also books that demand that our whole system be changed from top to bottom: books advocating socialism, or black nationalism and separatism. (Of course, books supportive of the government would be in the collection too.) But the fact that our libraries feel free to collect works which might be deemed subversive is itself an indication of how far we have come from the governmental control that many countries think normal and accept. I should not expect to find works critical of Kim Il Sung in the public library in Pyongyang, North Korea.

Freedom to read? Taken literally, without hindrance or exceptions, that's Whiggish, that's left, that's dangerous to duly constituted authority, that's as thunderingly revolutionary as one of General Washington's cannon. The freedom to read is not just the freedom to read candlelight romances; it isn't even just the freedom to read Kurt Vonnegut. It's the freedom to question authority, of parent, church and state, the freedom to take charge of your own body and your own life, the freedom to find out about Watergate, Koreagate, and Contragate; and it's all there at your local public or academic library. But the late Reagan Administration was more restrictive in the distribution of government information than any administration since the Second World War. Did Reagan's bureaucrats understand the potential social-change proclivities of free readers reading freely, and were they determined to put a stop to such goings-on?[53]

A colleague who advocates strict neutrality wrote me, "Why can't libraries just be libraries?" Because libraries are *libraries,* that's why, and an American library is a place for discovery and possible change. (The reader, of course, is perfectly free to read only books which support her own view, but the chance that she *might* read something that would upset her comfortable notions is inherent in the scope of our normal collecting—and it's a chance I personally delight in.) My neutrality colleague may have been more concerned with the statements of some state library associations, as well as those of the American Library Association, which do make a commitment to social change and responsibility. The Constitution, Bylaws, and other papers of ALA are full of recognitions of social responsibility, including commitments to affirmative action, special programs for Native Americans, and sanctions against the Republic of South Africa. (They also include professions of neutrality. As Swan indicates, the *Library Bill of Rights* is a "purist document"[54] with a lot of negatives built into it; I might add that it is really a bill of rights *for* the public and *against* librarians and some sectors of the public.) Some librarians may be disturbed by these passages committing the profession to social responsibility, but for me they are natural to a library's inherently troubling and challenging role in a democratic, "conservative-liberal" society. The Prince Regent and his admiral might be very upset if they could see what is going on today in the land they attempted to subjugate.

I am not advocating abandoning the well-balanced collection. If the collection is properly balanced, it offers at least the *potential* for progressive social change. I am only suggesting that a library association is not obliged, in the name of intellectual freedom, to offer space and time to a person who proposes to defend racist false-hoods or who has a reputation for so doing. That is to betray the empowering position of the library and of an association which sup-ports such libraries. Even if McCalden's books are held by a library, for reasons of study, or are available at some point through inter-library loan, a professional association has no obligation to give such an author a personal pulpit.

I prize highly the freedom to read, but I prize more highly the freedom to know; and I want to know that what I read is in some sense "so." Racism, pseudoscience, and government disinformation are antidemocratic, disheartening; they cheat, they betray, they make me feel unwell and dishonored. The democracy that I cherish is not just that of the town meeting and the school board election, valuable as these are: it is the democracy hoped for by Mary Dyer, Nathan Hale, Elijah Lovejoy, Medger Evers: men and women who gave their lives that you and I might take charge of our own. For me the concept of democracy is connected with individual self-determination, with dignity, and with mutual respect. This kind of freedom is connected with knowing, and *living* the truth, and not just with sifting conflicting opinions.

Part of the trouble we in America have in understanding free-dom is that we too often see it as a legal matter, isolated from other concerns. We appeal to courts and lawyers to settle rights and duties for us. Such an appeal is better than appealing to the whims of dic-tators or mobs, but we too easily assume that the judges and at-torneys have done all the work, and we can settle back and relax without worrying about the courts' decisions and the country's future. The Dred Scott decision affirmed slavery; the Thirteenth Amendment abolished it. In *Plessy* v. *Ferguson* we supported segregation; in *Brown* v. *Board of Education of Topeka* we de-nounced it. It was the judges who did these things, true, not the peo-ple, but the people acquiesced; they had not the vision of a John Woolman or a Martin Luther King, Jr., to stand up and say slavery and segregation are and were wrong, from beginning to end. We left that task to prophets, lawyers, and soldiers, and stowed the results of their labors in the history books and the legal codes. We have yet to see the day when bigotry will no longer be socially acceptable.

I hear an objection: you're describing a conformist society, Peattie, conformist for the left instead of the right. You're imposing a series of new taboos, as restrictive as the ones the reactionaries and "revisionists" would impose upon us. The point was made some years ago in a meeting of the New York Library Association, in which James A. Harvey, emphasizing the role of the library as a school for critical thinking, including material that some might find offensive, declared: "Bigots pay taxes; bigots use libraries; bigots read. Can public-supported libraries deny them the materials *they* find useful and valuable any more than librarians can deny works requested by blacks, women, Native Americans, Mexican-Americans, et al.?"[55]

Whether bigots read and use libraries is a moot question. But Harvey, who did not state what kind of material he wished to see included in a library that served bigots, seemed to ignore the fact that a bigot who came in and used the library might have his views changed. Can anyone doubt that this would be a change for the better in Mr. Bigot? Surely not. Yet our aim must not be to expel or erect taboos and barriers, but to persuade gently.

There is no question that pressure from below, as well as from peers, whether moral or physical, has frequently wreaked injustice on people who wished to maintain scholarly professionalism, of which they saw neutrality or objectivity as a vital component. Between 1955 and 1974 this country had more than its share of disruptive pressure tactics applied to universities, colleges, and their libraries. The story is told of the UCLA professor, not a Turk, who suggested that the number of Armenians killed by the Turks was greatly exaggerated, and who was hounded out of town. "Revisionist" historians have been forced out of teaching posts, as was Robert Faurisson in France.

Still, in the tension between popular pressure and academic freedom, historical truth and personal decency are our best guides. The number of Armenians killed by the Turks is variously quoted; "between 600,000 and 1,000,000 Armenians" says one source[56]; this must be compared with the figure of 1,110,000 Armenians alive in the census of 1896.[57] Under such circumstances, figures should be bracketed as high, middle, or low estimates. The Holocaust, however, happened not in the remote hinterlands of the Ottoman Empire but in the heart of Europe: while the Nazis burned many incriminating sheets of statistics, many survived, whether kept by Germans or partisans. We have fairly accurate records, at least in round numbers, for what occurred to the Jews in the towns and cities of Eastern Europe. These may be found in the appropriate entries in the *Encyclopedia Judaica,*[58] or in memoirs and other accounts in the voluminous literature.

Question a statistic? McCalden, or anyone, has the right to do that. But the denial of a huge mass of data, the lives and sufferings of millions, is not merely an exercise of freedom, not merely an eccentricity, but a lie to make further suffering possible.

The real point about the McCalden incident is not whether six million Jews and others died; or four million, or seven million. It is his use of the data to greatly diminish, to trivialize, and ultimately to justify, the Holocaust. Again, I come down to the question of personal integrity. It is not McCalden's questioning of conventional wisdom that makes him the enemy; I'm questioning traditional library wisdom right now. It is McCalden's antisemitism which he is concealing (though elsewhere he admits to being a racist).

Finally, it may be asked whether or not I am playing into the hands of the censors: whether this whole exercise has been what George Orwell called, on another occasion,[59] "a demonstration in favor of censorship." Swan has already anticipated this question in his essay, "Librarianship is censorship," cited above, and done so very well. My own avoidance of the term *censorship* is due to my perception that the word has been so abused that it can mean almost anything. A professor at Northwestern University says this of the term:

> *Censorship* is a word of many meanings. In its broadest sense it refers to suppression of information, ideas, or artistic expression by anyone, whether government officials, church authorities, private pressure groups, or speakers, writers, or artists themselves.

He goes on to explore its time, place, and manner; admits that in the legalistic sense censorship means only "the prevention by official government action of the circulation of messages already produced," but concludes,

> Yet all of these restraints have the effect of limiting the diversity that would otherwise be available in the marketplace of ideas and so may be considered censorship in its broadest sense.[60]

Here is a net so wide that it may catch alike the noble swan and the humble petty-fish. The definition is too broad, in that it not only ignores Swan's point, that the librarian is inevitably also a censor, but renders an exploration of the limits of toleration almost hopeless, if not meaningless. Some very eminent persons have discussed the limits of toleration[61] and they do not deserve to be treated as if they were a mixture of Torquemada, Josef Goebbels, Jerry Falwell and Pol Pot. To do so makes even invective feeble; "censorship" becomes a shibboleth to be applied by anyone to anyone. The accusation finally becomes an example of what it purports to decry: to tell someone he is a censor is to tell him to shut up.

A more serious charge is that the tradition of librarianship, as carried on by its noblest names, supports the libertarian side, and while eschewing invective, still regards any limits put on expression as approaching censorship, however that word may be defined or interpreted.

Let me answer this challenge with a personal note. I was, for the academic year 1960–1961, in the library school of the University of California, Berkeley, where the course on acquisitions was turned by its teacher and dean of the school, Professor LeRoy Merritt, into a class on intellectual freedom. No one who was there at the time can forget the way Merritt ranged his students in a circle, and engaged them in debate with himself and with each other. Eventually all of us were convinced that intellectual freedom, in its widest sense, must prevail over all considerations of private preference or public obloquy. I honor the memory of my decisive and eloquent teacher, who defended the presence of controversial books and periodicals of all kinds in libraries.

For some librarians, this confession will be the ultimate treason. To have been a student of LeRoy Merritt, and to have sunk so low as to imagine that there could be limits to toleration in selection for libraries, or any other professional activity! On the contrary, it is a tribute to my teacher that it took me so long to part company with a literal interpretation of his ideas. To those who would insist on literalism, here or elsewhere, I can only point out that a literal interpretation of any teacher's words, to the exclusion of any other interpretation or disagreement, would be censorship itself — as Merritt would surely have been the first to point out.

The libertarian tradition of librarianship, while it remains, and should remain, a living tradition, should not compel us to treat all intellectual freedom cases as exactly equal, and elicit from us the same knee-jerk response. To do that is to make us inflexible, and unable to act with decency and compassion when the need arises.

XIII.

I find, therefore, the traditional defenses of intellectual freedom in library work inadequate: the quest for truth in the marketplace of ideas, the sovereignty of the people through democracy, the slippery-slope argument, and the call for strict apolitical neutrality. It is time to set intellectual freedom on a sounder basis. To do this, I will have to champion Truth for the last time, by giving her a definition and a duty to perform.

A definition of truth would require a separate book, in which the theories of various philosophers were examined and refuted. Rather than this I will, at the risk of reasoning by analogy, follow Plato and go over into metaphor, if not myth. I liken Truth to the currency. In all ages and climes, as soon as people began to use money, the privilege of coining or printing money was reserved to the Crown. Counterfeiting, or the issuance of private money, was punished with extreme severity, and no philosopher or reformer has ever wished it otherwise. (The surest sign of the independence of a country is when it begins to strike its own coinage.) Although an individual may not know a particular truth, truth is the currency of the academy, of all educated, indeed honest, persons. We would no more sit and listen to a lying person (had we the power to find him such) than we would expect to find the Federal Reserve Board listening to the glib persuasions of a counterfeiter.

Truth, therefore, is something we all carry with us, as each morning we put cents, nickels, dimes, and quarters into our pockets, confident that they are lawful specie. We may not know, in the marketplace, the purchasing value of each coin; but for us, the truth-tellers, the one thing needful is that everyone in the market be handling no coin but the genuine.

In this view, Truth becomes not a question of epistemology, but of ethics. Reality shapes and determines our ethics. Truth becomes, in Hannah Arendt's word, coercive. This powerful coercion avoids subterfuge, decides debates, and calls to its aid witnesses and historians close to their sources. With Walt Whitman, it says, "I was the man, I suffer'd, I was there." Not just equal time, but a single standard: this Truth demands. Closer to the prophets than to the persuaders, it speaks, as it did of old, with authority, not as the scribes.

Meanwhile, the Librarian, as teller of truths, does not stand alone. We have noted dignity, equality and mutual respect as concomitants of intellectual freedom, and we might add to these, justice and nonviolence. We might even (were there time) paint a picture of the free Librarian, as one who perceives that her freedom to read and select does not exist in isolation, but is bound up with other virtues and concerns.

Such a Librarian would understand that the best defense of intellectual freedom is one in which freedom to read and investigate is part of a network of virtues we call civilization. That word is loaded: and I know it. It means a society in which freedom is joined with, and makes possible, justice, compassion, dignity, and peace. Through this union we know ourselves and our neighbors: our history and theirs, our rights, duties and concerns, and theirs. This civilization does not prevail now; but it does exist here and there, in (among other places, sometimes) libraries. It exists wherever Truth is upheld and defended against all calumny. We want to know the truth in order to be free, and we want to be free in order to be good.

I started out to find flaws in the traditional defenses of intellectual freedom without destroying intellectual freedom itself. Investigation led me to seek not only a different foundation for intellectual freedom, but to find a new way of being a citizen: one who does not see himself or herself as being bound by *this* Supreme Court decision, nor being loosed by *that* one, but rather entwined into a network of intellectual responsibility, in which truth, freedom, decency, compassion and personal integrity, guide his or her steps in every aspect of professional work, and in public as well as private life.

XIV.

Now at the last, a kraken arises from the depths, posing a question it has posed to every moralist since Plato: who is to enforce this integrity? How is the corruption of a whole society, and of typical individuals, prefigured in the *Republic* (VIII 543–IX 575) and actually carried out in twentieth-century Germany and Austria, to be avoided? What is to prevent any librarian, or association of librarians, from selling out to corruption in the name of freedom, compromise, weakness of will?

The answer can only be given in the personal integrity of each individual, supported by the sense of good order of others in the same profession, so that no one is dependent on herself alone, but all are critical of each other. (This assumes that even a librarian working alone reads the professional literature and goes to as many conferences as he can!) And only a close reading of empirical truths, a study of history and science, an understanding of politics, and a devotion to speaking truth as the only acceptable currency of discourse, can prevent fundamental distortion of reality, compromise and expediency from assaulting the honor of any company of librarians. That this may require serious study, shared expertise, is a burden for the profession to take up. But that this effort amounts to censorship, I cannot allow. If a librarian acquires a contrafactual book, an "untruth," she may do so for a number of reasons, but they had all better be good ones. "Access" may not be reason good enough *by itself*.

The answer to the kraken's challenge, then, becomes one of individual decision. The librarian must be able to stand up and say that the speaker you are about to hear is using your own defenses against you; is asking you to lend an ear to something that is false, and proved false by many witnesses. Further, if this speaker came to power, she would suppress you first among her victims, precisely on account of your neutrality. To speak out against racism, therefore, is not just an exercise in intellectual freedom, but an act which expresses freedom's very essence, the dignity and truth inherent in every individual.

Hear now the conclusion of the whole matter. McCalden's case against the California Library Association failed, but the whole library profession owes a vote of thanks to David McCalden, for having penetrated its weak traditional defenses. He has shown us that we need to have a comprehensive view of intellectual freedom as bound up with other values. Otherwise, we are liable not only to charges of racism and other forms of discrimination, but our own professional rhetoric, our own *Library Bill of Rights,* can be turned against us. We need to settle our defenses on strong foundations: logical, self-critical, free of prejudice; and we need to know the truth about our world. We need to know that the world is real, is round; that a terrible and specific thing happened to six million Jews; and that the freedom we celebrate today was won for us by men and women who perceived the truths that others were afraid to face. To them, and to all modern librarians everywhere, I offer my defense.

References

1. For an overview of this professional activity and a critique of its success in recent years, see Noel Peattie, "Intellectual freedom activism in the sixties: the defense of a professional standard," in: *Activism in American librarianship, 1962-1973,* edited by Frederick Stielow and Mary Lee Bundy (New York, Greenwood, 1987), p. [43]-58.

2. See, for example, the interview with the late Bradford Chambers, editor of *Interracial books for children bulletin,* in *Sipapu,* v. 13, no. 2, consecutive issue no. 26, p. 1-15. For a coverage of the American Library Association-sponsored film, *The speaker,* see *Sipapu,* v. 8, no. 2 (consec. issue no. 16), p. 17-18; v. 9, no. 1 (c.i. 17), p. 14-15, 17-20; v. 9, no. 2 (c.i. 18), p. 7-9, 20.

3. Some of this information is derived from McCalden himself, in material supplied by his group, Truth Missions, which he apparently formed after leaving the Institute for Historical Review, which he had founded. Material regarding his subsequent activities, including the proposed but abandoned conference at Pomona College, may be obtained from *Response,* v. 11, August 1985, the newsletter of the Simon Wiesenthal Foundation, Los Angeles.

4. The literature on this incident is considerable. The most comprehensive chronology is in the California Library Association *Newsletter,* v. 27, no. 1, January 1985. A fair account was written by Susan Kamm, "'Holocaust hoax' publisher barred..." in *American libraries,* v. 16, no. 1, January 1985, p. 5-7. A running history is provided in *Sipapu,* v. 16, no. 1 (consecutive no. 31), p. 17-21, and v. 16, no. 2 (c.i. 32), p. 8-16. McCalden has assembled a fine collection of newspaper clippings, plus his own chronology, in his *Revisionists' reprints,* issue #8, January 1985; at that time available from P.O. Box 3849, Manhattan Beach CA 90266; he reproduces material from both sides of the issue. See also: Mark Elliott and Michael McClintock, "Holocaust 'revisionists' and the California Library Association," *Midstream,* v. 32, no. 4, April 1986, p. 36-38; and following on that, "Letters," from Jeff Selth and David McCalden, and "Reply," *Midstream,* v. 32, no. 9, November 1986, p. 59-60. Grant Burns has an editorial, "Well, shut my mouth," in *New pages,* issue #9, p. 3 (1985).

   McCalden also desired to exhibit with COSMEP, the international association of small publishers, and joined COSMEP in order to do so. The resultant division of opinion evoked a protest from Sanford Berman, and one COSMEP Board member, John Crawford, resigned in anger. The later pages of the *Sipapu* articles referred to above cover this subject briefly. COSMEP had previously had an encounter with a publisher whose title was considered sexist, and who only withdrew his book from their book van under considerable pressure. Since anyone who joins COSMEP is entitled to all the rights and privileges of the organization, and since there are no qualifications, other than being "small," for joining COSMEP, the issue of "offensive literature" might well return to COSMEP.

5. John Swan, "Untruth or consequences," *Library journal,* v. 111, no. 12, July 1986, p. 44-52. This article is reprinted in the present book.

6. *Ibid.,* p. 48.

7. [Noel Peattie] "Cardinal Mazarin is dead?!" *Sipapu,* v. 17, no. 2, consec. issue no. 34, p. 11-17.

8. See McCalden's letter, quoted in *Midstream,* November 1986, p. 59.

9. The most recent life of Norton is by William Drury: *Norton I, Emperor of the United States,* foreword by Melvin Belli, New York, Dodd, Mead, 1986.

10. Swan, *Lj,* p. 51.

11. *Sipapu,* v. 16, no. 2 (consec. issue 32), p. 9.

12. *Ibid.,* p. 13-14.

13. *American libraries,* v. 19, no. 8, September 1988, p. 640.

14. Swan, *Library journal*, v. 111, no. 12, p. 44–52. Page references will hereafter be given in text.
15. For an account of Voliva, see Martin Gardner, *Fads and fallacies in the name of science* (New York, Dover, 1957), p. 16–19. Please notice that I have no objections to the Joshua Nortons and Wilbur Volivas; they are history's harmless eccentrics; they may address any library conferences as they like, without my hindrance.
16. See "The heart of darkness," an annotated bibliography of radical right publications and those of right-watchers, in *New pages,* no. 9 [1985], p. 1, 6–13.
17. Robert Edward Herzstein, *The war that Hitler won* (New York, Putnam's, 1978), Introduction, p. 22.
18. *Sipapu,* v. 16, no. 2 (consec. no. 32), p. 11.
19. Harry G. Frankfurt, *The importance of what we care about: philosophical essays* (Cambridge University Press, 1988). Chapter 10: "On bullshit," p. 117–133. See also Joel Achenbach, "Creeping surrealism: does anybody really know what's real anymore?" in *Utne reader,* Nov.–Dec. 1988, p. 112–116.
20. See the article by Gertrude Ezorsky, "Pragmatic theory of truth," in *Encyclopedia of philosophy* (Macmillan, 1967), v. 6, p. 427–430.
21. Handlin, *Truth in history* (Cambridge, Mass.: Belknap Press/Harvard, 1979), Chapter 6, "An instance of criticism," p. 150.
22. This recalls the disputes in the library literature about how to classify "creation science" books, and the works of Carlos Castaneda. Hennepin County Library's Sanford Berman (correctly, I think) placed the one in religion and the other in fiction—much to the dismay of the partisans of both texts.
23. Hannah Arendt, "Truth and politics," in *Political theory and social change,* ed. with an introduction by David Spitz (New York, Atherton Press, 1967), p. [3] 27. These papers were initially read at the annual meeting of the American Political Science Association in 1960, and apparently 1967 saw the first appearance of Arendt's essay in print.
24. Hugh Thomas, *The Spanish Civil War* (New York, Harper, 1963; there is a later edition).
25. Bernard Lewis, *History: remembered, recovered, invented* (Princeton, 1975).
26. Paul Chevigny, *More speech: dialogue rights and modern liberty* (Philadelphia, Temple University Press, 1988).
27. For a short description of this case, which upheld the "bad tendency" principle, see *Academic American encyclopedia,* v. 9, p. 121.
28. Sanford Berman, *Prejudices and antipathies* (Metuchen, N.J.: Scarecrow Press, 1971).
29. *Echoes from the Holocaust: philosophical reflections on a dark time,* ed. by Alan Rosenberg and Gerald E. Myers (Philadelphia, Temple University Press, 1988).
30. *Echoes,* ch. 2, Rainer C. Baum, "Holocaust: moral indifference as *the* form of modern evil" (p. 53–89).
31. *Ibid.,* p. 71 and p. 84.
32. *Echoes,* ch. 4, Laurence Thomas, "Liberalism and the Holocaust" (p. 105–117), p. 108.
33. *Echoes,* ch. 6, Martin P. Golding, "On the idea of moral pathology," p. 128–148.
34. *Ibid.,* p. 141.
35. P.G.J. Pulzer, *The rise of political anti-semitism in Germany and Austria* (New York, Wiley, 1964) (New dimensions in history; essays in political history). For a summary of antisemitism in Europe in the years preceding 1914, see the article "AntiSemitism" in *Encyclopaedia Britannica,* 11th edition (Cambridge University Press, 1912), p. 134–146. The article is signed by Lucien Wolf, vice-president of the Jewish Historical Society of England, and is optimistic in its conclusions. I hope that Mr. Wolf did not live to see 1933.

36. Max Weinrich (1894–1969), *Hitler's professors: the part of scholarship in Germany's crimes against the Jewish people* (New York, Yiddish Scientific Institute [YIVO], 1946).
37. Benno Müller-Hill, *Murderous science: elimination by scientific selection of Jews, Gypsies, and others, Germany 1933–1945,* translated by George R. Fraser (Oxford University Press, 1988).
38. Müller-Hill, *Murderous science:* "Nine questions," p. [88]–104. The final "Warning" should be read carefully, in view of the world's headlines since 1945.
39. John Stuart Mill, *On liberty,* ed. by Elizabeth Rapaport (Indianapolis, Hackett, 1978), ch. 1, "Introductory," p. 9.
40. Mill, *On liberty,* Rapaport ed., ch. 2, "Of the liberty of thought and discussion," p. 16.
41. For a discussion of the political aspects of creationism, see William J. Bennetta, *Crusade of the credulous: a collection of articles about contemporary creationism and the effects of that movement on public education* (San Francisco, California Academy of Sciences Press, 1986).
42. See also Sanford Berman, "'In the beginning': the creationist agenda," in *Library journal,* October 15, 1985, p. 31–34.
43. Thomas Scanlon, "A theory of freedom of expression," *Philosophy and public affairs,* v. 1, no. 2, winter 1972, p. [204]–226.
44. United States Constitution, Article 1, Section 6, paragraph 1.
45. Frederick Schauer, *Free speech: a philosophical enquiry* (Cambridge University Press, 1982), p. 3.
46. On the influence of television on rational thinking, see Neil Postman, "The contradictions of freedom of information," in: *Alternative library literature, 1986–1987: a biennial anthology,* ed. by Sanford Berman and James P. Danky (Jefferson, N.C., McFarland, 1988), p. 37–49.
47. *A critique of pure tolerance,* by Robert Paul Wolff, Barrington Moore, Jr., and Herbert Marcuse (Boston, Beacon Press, 1965).
48. Marcuse, in *A critique of pure tolerance,* p. 85.
49. One good summary of the early stages of the Rushdie affair appears in *Newsweek,* Feb. 27, 1989, p. 34–39.
50. John C. Swan, "Librarianship is censorship," *Library journal,* v. 104, no. 17 (October 1, 1979), p. 2040–2043.
51. R.B. Nye and J.E. Morpurgo, *A history of the United States* (Harmondsworth, Penguin, 1955), v. 1, p. 307.
52. James Pack, *The man who burned the White House: Admiral Sir James Cockburn, 1772–1853* (Annapolis, Naval Institute Press, 1987), ch. 1, p. 13–20. After all, American troops had (contrary to orders) burned the Parliament buildings and library at York (now Toronto), then the capital of Canada. Jefferson, who restored the holdings of the Library of Congress with his own collection, described the arson at Washington as an act of barbarism. When Cockburn retired from the Royal Navy, he held four successive seats in Parliament for the Tories, and showed himself no vigorous defender of democratic reform.
53. For a clipping file of government disinformation and suppression of information, see: Data Center, Oakland, Calif., *The right to know,* preface by Zoia Horn (Oakland, 1986).
54. Swan, "Librarianship is censorship," p. 2043.
55. James A. Harvey, "Acting for the children," *Library journal,* v. 98, February 1971, p. 602–605 (= *School library journal,* v. 18, November 1971, p. 10–11).
56. *Academic American encyclopedia* (New York, Grolier, 1987), v. 2, p. 172.
57. *Encyclopaedia Britannica,* 11th edition (Cambridge, England, 1912), v. 27, p. 426.

58. *Encyclopedia Judaica* (New York, Macmillan, 1972).
59. George Orwell, "The prevention of literature," in *Selected essays* (Harmondsworth, England, Penguin, 1957), p. 159.
60. Franklyn S. Haiman, article "censorship," in: *Academic American encyclopedia,* 1987, v. 4, p. 246.
61. See, for example: *Aspects of toleration: philosophical studies,* edited by John Horton and Susan Mendus (London, Methuen, 1985); *On toleration,* edited by Susan Mendus and David Edwards (Oxford, Clarendon Press, 1987); *Justifying toleration: conceptual and historical perspectives,* edited by Susan Mendus (Cambridge, England, Cambridge University Press, 1988).

Damned Lies, Part II:
A Rebuttal in Specifics

John Swan

At the opening of the Vatican Archives to the broad community of historians and other scholars in 1883, Pope Leo XIII declared that "the first law of history is not to dare to utter falsehood; the second, not to fear to speak the truth."[1] This is an assertion to which I and, I assume, all other civil libertarians (certainly including J.S. Mill) would assent. In my other contributions to our debate and to this volume, I thought I had made clear that there is nothing in the imperative of absolute intellectual tolerance that contradicts a commitment to the truth. However, I seem to have overestimated the lucidity of my prose, and some attempt to clarify my position and to correct what I take to be misrepresentations thereof is in order.

One apparent misinterpretation that has large consequences to Noel Peattie's angle of attack is that committed upon a particular passage in my original *Library Journal* "Untruth" piece. The passage, quoted by Noel, is what I regard as a thoroughly unoriginal assertion of the essential subjectivity in our individual and collective relationships with reality:

> ...the real world offers us a multiplicity of "truths" [note the quotation marks around the word; my opponent properly included them, but apparently didn't find them significant] compounded of desirability and appearance, often contradictory, sometimes in violent conflict with one another. As human beings we inevitably hold cause with one or many of these truths, but as librarians our cause

is, in a very practical sense, not truth but freedom. Indeed our truth
is freedom, freedom of access....[2]

The first part of this statement has numberless predecessors,
from Plato through Kant to Wittgenstein to now, but my opponent
takes it as an occasion for a reproof on the subject of confusing appearance with the *Ding an sich:* "The real world does not 'offer' us
anything . . . it simply *is.* . . . 'Don't confuse the finger pointing at the
moon, with the moon itself.'" And not only do I believe, according
to Peattie, that the universe offers us meanings on a platter, but I
am apparently naive enough to believe that everyone understands
the content of that platter, because he finds it necessary to remind
us that

> the librarian, in collecting this mélange, can only hope, not know,
> that the reader has enough education, patience, and discernment,
> to engage in the sorting process and come out with the "right"
> answer. But even educated people have their prejudices; you can
> hear them at any Faculty Club.

Well, yes, we certainly hope that the patron of our stores of information will be able to exercise critical intelligence and discover
in them what is actually there—whatever that means—but the
"right" answer? Surely this is a hope only sustainable, only relevant,
in certain limited (if large) realms of inquiry. To such questions as
"What is the capital of Maine?" or "Is the earth flat?" or "Is it true
that six million Jews died at the hands of the Nazis?" we can assert
that there is such an unequivocal answer and insist that our libraries
will provide it. But the world of bare fact, as essential as it is to all
understanding, is subsumed in the individual mind by a realm much
more resistant to consensus. For instance, there are interpreters of
the Holocaust who grant its occurrence but view it as a regrettable
but understandable response to the threat of Stalinist communism;
they may well be arranging the facts to suit a "hidden agenda" more
sinister than that of those who deny them altogether, and they are
certainly more influential.

The point of this restatement of the obvious (the implications
of which can be much more rewardingly examined in the works of
Karl Popper and the other lights of modern epistemology, as well
as in those of the immortals mentioned two paragraphs above) is not
that Noel doesn't already know it. Rather, it is that he builds a case

against libertarians of a (relatively) purist stripe on the assumption that *we* don't understand that information can be misinterpreted, that lies can be dangerous. In fact, no serious argument for freedom of access can be based on a simple belief that, in any given context, the "right" answer will prevail, even in situations where there is such a thing, even when it ought to be unmistakable.

Once having decided that I (and other libertarians) have fallen into errors of such appalling simplicity, Peattie proceeds to set the record straight with his own "taxonomy," and his own schemata of truths, untruths, lies, the Big Lie — all in the service of a vision that, as genuinely admirable as it is, is fundamentally very simple in itself: We should all shun dangerous falsehoods and embrace healthy truths. This urge for moral and epistemological decisiveness seems to be the impulse underlying all of his arguments. It is bracing, at times, in the face of the eternal wash of ambiguity that confronts us in the information business, but despite its claim to the contrary, it has its own impractical strains, some of which are themselves dangerous to the practice of real intellectual freedom in real social and political environments.

Although his own record as writer and activist in the real world argues that he agrees with the civil libertarian position that there is a fundamental, if sometimes blurred, distinction between words and deeds, Peattie attempts to place certain words in the category of deeds. There is strong precedent for this, of course, in the Supreme Court decisions which removed words posing "a clear and present danger" (Holmes' famous phrase for the majority in *Schenck* v. *U.S.*), "fighting words," and certain other forms of expression, also specifically named but vaguely defined, from under the First Amendment umbrella (pornography in *Miller* and child pornography in *Ferber* are particularly troublesome examples). But Peattie is even more ambitious; he wants to distinguish harmless delusions from dangerous lies, to cast words uttered in the service of the Big Lie out of the environs of free discourse.

Peattie believes that "to describe any part of" the history of Jewish experience of violent injustice at the hands of Gentiles, "including the period of their last and greatest suffering, as false, is not merely to question a statistic, but to attempt to brainwash a population — to commit a kind of 'genocide by false history.'" It is certainly true that to use words to incite a riot against Jews, or anyone else, is the equivalent of Justice Holmes' most famous words-as-deeds example, shouting "Fire!" in a crowded theater, as history's countless *Kristallnachts* have demonstrated. But to express the opinion that the Holocaust did not occur, however malicious the intent of the argument, is not in itself "brainwashing" anyone, and it is not genocide of any kind. To commit this sort of confusion is to confuse words and deeds, to stretch the "bad tendency" argument into dangerous reaches of sweeping censorship, putting at risk all of history's abundant evidence of writings against the Jews. The Holocaust-hoaxers are but the latest manifestation of a long tradition of anti–Jewish paranoia.

We may not want the Papal exhortations to First Crusaders to kill Jews on the way to the Holy Land to exist, but the words do exist, just as did the pogroms which they incited. They, and the words of Rosenberg, Hitler, McCalden, are part of the context of history, and if we have any hope for understanding that history, or ourselves, they belong within the boundaries of free communication. Again, this is no different from Noel's basic position concerning tolerance, but in drawing a distinction between the documents of the history of antisemitic violence and arguments which deny that history, even while asserting that the latter are in fact further manifestations of the former, he is trying to establish a boundary for that tolerance that has no logical existence.

The license for drawing this line seems to come, at least in part, from his distrust of the "shibboleth" that "Freedom for what we like includes freedom for what we detest" because "freedom is indivisible." He asks, "Who said it was? If it is indivisible, what principle of unity holds it together?" He implies that the statement is an expression of unthinking impracticality. The *locus classicus* of the idea is, once again, Justice Holmes, in *U.S.* v. *Schwemmer:*

> If there is any principle of the Constitution that more imperatively calls for attachment than any other it is the principle of free thought — not free thought for those who agree with us, but freedom for the thought that we hate.

These are not the words of a man with a thoughtlessly naive notion of what tolerance for the detestable idea implies. He demonstrated a lifelong awareness — he was in his late eighties at the time of the *Schwemmer* decision (1928) — that the necessary practical restraints upon free expression did not affect the fundamental logic of the indivisibility of freedom. It is not "held together" by anything, any more than is the concept of truth, another unitary concept which, despite that essential indivisibility, is buffeted by change, restraint, re-, mis-, over-, and under-interpretation in its manifestations in the real world.

To grant freedom for expression we find acceptable and to deny it for that which we don't is to betray the concept as a whole, not divide it into components; that which is acceptable doesn't encounter resistance in the first place, and it is only in resistance that the notion of freedom is tested. Obviously we all, libertarians and otherwise, "betray" the concept to the extent that we impose an array of restraints upon all of our freedoms, including the freedom of expression, for more or less sound practical reasons arising from the limitations in human nature. This is one of the basic costs of civilization, and, of course, denying freedom for certain kinds of expression and action protects the existence of other freedoms within society. But it should be recognized as just that, a necessary cost in practice, not a flaw in the fundamental principle.

It is ironic, in this regard, that Peattie chose to cast "fiction" out of his "taxonomy of texts" in which the fact/truth content is relevant to his arguments. These days it is precisely in this area that freedom of expression is most severely tested and the indivisible essence of that freedom most urgently demonstrated. A bitter clash of religions and cultures has resulted in Salman Rushdie's words of fiction being defined by representatives of one beleaguered culture as deeds of blasphemy punishable by death. Those who would ban the book (even if they would spare its author) on the grounds that it offends the sensibilities of those who find in it (or about it — the vast majority of its attackers having no firsthand knowledge of what is actually in it) an attack upon Islam would do well to look further into freedom's necessary indivisibility.

There is no question that many works of fiction as well as nonfiction, great and small, give offense, real offense, to many different groups; to decide that silencing the offenders is proper recourse, rather than replying to them, exposing them, or ignoring them, as the occasion warrants, is to give license for a general silence. They who find offense in Shakespeare, Lawrence, *Birth of a Nation,* "The Miller's Tale," *Portnoy's Complaint, The Last Temptation of Christ,* are waiting, not very patiently, in the wings.

There is much in my worthy opponent's discourse on the subject of variously false expression and the toleration thereof that is in itself worth pondering, but which I find beside the point of our relatively narrow range of real disagreement, largely because of the above-described problems with his notion of the nature of freedom. He summons the likes of Harry Frankfurt and Oscar Handlin in their different but equally vigorous refusals to suffer knaves and fools (and liars and bullshitters). The suggestion is that we civil libertarians, in our opposition to any authority which claims to dictate the truth to others, have a quarrel with those who insist on the importance of discerning and defending the truth. We don't; none whatever — unless Noel is suggesting that Oscar Handlin believes that we should substitute censorship of liars for the exercise of our individual integrity and powers of discrimination in exposing them, in which case I suggest a careful rereading of his sources.

It seems to me that Handlin's frustration with the fact that librarians classify revisionist Williams's work as history rather than fiction is nothing more than exasperation rather of the kind that Thomas Jefferson expended upon the hostile press; I don't see either of them proposing that a higher authority tell either librarians or journalists what to do with their material — within certain categories of expression, that is: I should concede at this point that there are whole realms of libel and fraud which present at their borders such no-man's-lands of disputed territory that there is little agreement even among libertarians. Indeed, Jefferson (along with most of his founding confreres) was quite positive on the point that government — state government as opposed to federal authority (that for him was the chief flaw in the Sedition Act) — *did* have the right to restrain "the overwhelming torrent of slander which is confounding all vice and virtue, all truth and falsehood in the US."[3] I suspect, in fact, that Noel and I would agree that, for all the necessity of such restraint, the current libel law often works to the advantage of self-protective officials and other figures in power, rather than to the advancement of the truth.

But to return to our disagreements, or at least differences, we have a number in our understanding of the etiology of the Nazi disease, one or two of which are worth mentioning. As I understand it, the point of the extensive Peattie excursus on the corruption of the German intelligentsia (along with most everyone else) by the promulgators of evil and tellers of lies is that this phenomenon — true and terrible as it was — demonstrates some basic weakness, a fatal naivete, in the civil libertarian position:

> At this point, readers, we have touched the nadir of the libertarian conscience. We have discovered that there is no constitution that

cannot be rewritten, that no outworn prejudice can be completely eradicated, that no amount of education can resist all social pressures and make its doctors incorruptible.

The "libertarian conscience" can, I suppose, be a Pollyannaish thing in the right — make that wrong — minds, but there is no logical necessity for civil libertarians in particular to be accused of this blindness to the boundless capacity of our species for evil and self-deception. Indeed, the civil libertarian position is based on a faith in the human mind to find its way in the (heavily qualified) "market-place of ideas." But that is not the same thing as a lack of awareness that the human mind may well not find its way, or may be seduced by the wrong ideas. It is nothing more than the same fundamental, if wary, faith in human critical faculties that makes possible any belief in democracy — including, I am certain, that of the proven libertarian activist Noel Peattie.

This is true despite the fact that he describes as a "dodge" the act of recommending that a student who asks whether a Holocaust-hoax book is true go "Read it, read some other material over there, and make up your own mind!" This "dodge" is, or ought to be, the inevitable expression of the above-mentioned faith in capacity of the freely informed mind to make better decisions than that which has only half the story. Noel and I would agree that at this point the librarian is also free, as a professional as well as a morally aware person, to share with that student his own informed point of view. But I do not believe that it is a mere "dodge" to offer the patron the detestable as well as the acceptable points of view, and again I suspect that as a matter of practical librarianship both Noel and I would offer as many different points of view, even in the area of the Holocaust, as our resources would reasonably allow.

Without dwelling drearily on his exposition of the Millian position, I'll assert that here, too, he underestimates the capacity for imagining powerful lies in the libertarian vision. In his defense of the Mormons (see the Mill entry in my bibliography) and in many other arguments for the broadening of public tolerance, Mill demonstrated that ideas can be dangerous and still the risk of tolerance is better than the act of intolerance. Yes, his faith that in the long run the most powerful ideas are those aligned with truth was less troubled and qualified than ours, but his was a different age — an age in which social philosophers such as Mill did indeed prepare the way for laws protecting the wilderness and wildlife, all in the name of a greater human good. Mill had his limitations (as Noel's use of Schauer indicates), which are as much a part of the libertarian traditions — and its dilemmas — as his central arguments. But as far as I can tell, the essential riskiness of human nature, the central feature of most of those dilemmas, is not a problem solved by any of his critics, either.

But rather than continue to pick away, let me focus on the major misunderstandings (as I understand them) and try to recast the terms of the debate (as I debate them). Much of his argument relies on the distinction between the mere "untruth" and the *"lie"*: "I define," says Peattie, "a *lie* as a deliberate falsehood uttered to deceive and hurt people, by a person who really knows the truth but deliberately denies or distorts it." I have no quarrel with this, as far as it goes (although it certainly is not adequate to what is actually a complex subject — see, for example, Sissela Bok[4]). But it is apparently my opponent's ambition to use this distinction to construct policy.

This calls for a good deal of the will-to-be-decisive noted above, and therefore some clearing away of the underbrush. People who lie out of a "passionate need to believe something," including "alcoholics [and] the . . . mentally ill" are forgiven, at least not included in the category of deliberate liars, and Big Liars, who ought to be shunned by the guardians of healthy discourse. This is a sincerity test, despite the fact that a few lines further on Noel makes short work of the "sincerity" of Hitler and other antisemites, on the grounds that some lies are, in effect, just too big and too iniquitous to let their tellers off the hook. Thus, Swan's "untruth" becomes a "euphemism."

This would be scanned. A euphemism for what? For the utterances of insincere and malicious people? We should police the world and our library conferences for signs of malice and dangerous insincerity? I'll admit these qualities are present in abundance in the world, certainly including library conferences, but I have no idea how one would go about this — or who would 'scape whipping if we tried. Yes, Peattie's concern is rightly for the Big Lie and the words and ideas that contain the seeds of racism, sexism, genocide, but all the will to clarity in the world is not going to sort one sort of malicious lie from another according to some standard of danger potential, even among those lies with a proven record of bloodletting behind them. Some people who harbor racist hatreds are harmless fools; some are dangerous criminals. The content of the racist idea is not, in itself, going to reveal which is which.

It is obvious enough that disputes over fact and disputes over morality are different things, but in practical, legal, and psychological reality, they are actually not so far apart as all that. Just as Doctor Johnson tried to dismiss the subjective universe of Bishop Berkeley by kicking a rock, Peattie seeks to expose lies with a universe of solid, verifiable *facts*. As positive as they both are, neither gesture takes us very far into the labyrinth of the human imagination — and it is precisely there that these different universes of discourse meet. As I argued originally, there are many who *know* that abortion is murder with the same certainty that most of us *know* that the Holocaust occurred. Yes, it is true that the fact of the Holocaust has been verified in countless objective ways not available to the right-to-lifers, but in the moral imagination that is a distinction without a difference: every image of a developing fetus is verification enough for them. And for many of those who deny the Holocaust, the greater the amount of evidence confuting their position, the larger and more sinister the conspiracy fabricating that evidence.

And there is an even more problematic issue: If a lie is "a deliberate falsehood uttered . . . by a person who really knows the truth," what about those who, for whatever reason of blindness or pathology, really believe that the Holocaust did not occur? As Sissela Bok has pointed out, the nature of self-deception has been a problem since Plato[5], and for many it isn't even a matter of self-deception: antisemitism and racism are cultural forces that can shape "reality" so strongly that it does not occur to most of those who have grown up within that "reality" ever to question it (this is one of the dark lessons of the harrowing documentary series on the Holocaust, *Shoah*). The Peattiean dispensation for crazies and drunks is simply not adequate clarification in this matter.

We can all agree that some things are true and some are false, and we can even agree (*pace* George Berkeley) that there is a reality out there independent of our mental information processors. But that hardly serves to ensure a consensus as to just which things are true and which are false, which statements are reflections of reality and which are distortions. The problem is in the processing: Does my truth-defending antagonist believe that all those who deny the existence of the Holocaust are deliberate liars? That all those who believe that blacks are inferior are really in possession of the truth, but determined "to deceive and hurt people" with intentional lies? Would that we could define our enemies so simply, but I will grant my opposition the assumption that he knows better.

But if some—many, maybe most—of those who promulgate lies such as these actually believe them themselves, how are they to be treated under the Peattie policy? If we dismiss the absurdity that we can look into people's minds and administer a sincerity test, the implication is that we treat them as if they were deliberate liars. We cast them out of the public discourse; we do not argue with them because they should know better, and because the ideas they promote are harmful, dangerous *lies*. And, according to the Peattie argument, we "neutral" librarians have not dared, in our misguided valuelessness, to come out and say, "That book is a lie."

The Peattie Revolution will change all that, and whether its perpetrators and followers actually swallow its contents, "that book is a lie," and out it goes—well, no, not necessarily "out": the actual details of theoretical Peattiean intolerance are sufficiently troubled by the actual long and honorable practice of Peattiean libertarianism that the practical outlines of the former are unclear. We can refuse the liars and cheats a place in our programs, but we will get their books—sometimes, when people want them, or might want them, and we will tell people the books are the work of scoundrels, sometimes, if they ask, maybe if they don't; we will represent the full spectrum of ideas and information, but we won't support scoundrels, or not very much, depending on their places in the spectrum, and how dangerous their ideas are to other ideas in said spectrum.

I grant that more sympathetic readers might glean a clearer sense of the practical implications of Noel's argument for virtuous intolerance than I suggest here, but for me the fuzzy outlines and ambiguities are strikingly similar to those of the civil libertarian position: as I suggest elsewhere, translating the tolerance of all ideological positions into actual practice means tolerating some things and not tolerating others. Borrowing, again, from myself in another source, in reference to the controversy over the Edmonton Library's acquisition of large numbers of works denying the Holocaust, "though we acknowledge the ambiguities in the notion of a 'balanced' collection, we do not, as professionals, interpret it to mean that we are constrained to buy as many lies about the Holocaust as truths."

Peattie insists on associating civil libertarianism with a single philosophy above all others, pragmatism—a rather impoverished version thereof, at that. He argues, in essence, that the toleration of lies must be based on a philosophy which denies any particular standing to truth, except as facts corroborated by evidence. Or, since we intellectual freedom purists grant liars a right to debate, we must therefore believe that truth itself is subject to debate. Although a defense of pragmatist/instrumentalist philosophy is not to the point here, I feel it necessary to express a warning that the summary, and particularly the conclusion in total relativism, given by Noel in his original *Sipapu* criticism[6] of my *Library Journal* version of libertarianism is totally inadequate to the subtlety and power of the enterprise. There is still a fairly broad consensus that the work of Peirce, James and Dewey constitutes the core of the most important American contribution to the critique of metaphysics and to rational philosophical inquiry as a whole. If you'll forgive a not entirely irrelevant extension to this tangent, let me quote from Arthur Murphy, one of pragmatism's most cogent critics:

> Their insistence that the meaning and worth of ideas is rightly judged, not by their conformity to a "reality" set up in advance as the final standard of truth and reasonableness, but by the way they function in the context of responsible inquiry, was both revolutionary and salutary. Pragmatism did not, as its enthusiasts supposed, give us a new meaning for truth, but it did help enormously to show us where to look for the truth that is reliably attainable, and how to know it when we see it. Its emphasis on the plurality of contexts in which ideas can function significantly, and on the importance, if we would make our ideas clear, of interpreting them specifically by reference to their use and function in such contexts, is, in my judgment, the greatest single contribution to critical philosophy of our time.[7]

Noel has revised a good deal of his attack on pragmatism out of his position paper, another reason that I need not go on at length on the subject, but I believe that Murphy's tribute is useful here as a reminder that our liberal and libertarian forebears established patterns of research and vision that, however flawed, have provided us with a heritage of breadth and clarity — and curiosity — that insists that no corner of the human mind is so dark that we ought to deny it the illumination of inquiry and communication.

And one more pragmatic item, this stemming from Noel's treatment of Dewey in the aforementioned *Sipapu* article. It is quite true that in his ambition to tie the definition of truth to empirical verification, Dewey ran into trouble. According to his scheme, if something is neither true nor false, in an absolute sense, until it is known, then it must be regarded as in a state of being neither true nor false, which is a violation of the law of the excluded middle. A proposition must indeed be at all times true or not true, and Dewey's error was, in effect, to project an impossible "middle" state by conflating the state of being true with the process of ascertaining that something is true. It was a fairly simple error, not shared by Peirce or James, not insignificant because it does relate to other limitations of pragmatism, but hardly the fatal flaw in the whole effort, and not by any means sufficient pretext for boiling that effort down into the flaccid relativism described in Peattie's argument.

The point of flogging this particular dead horse, or dead Cardinal, is not to defend pragmatism—the tenets of the philosophy have nothing in particular to do with the defense of tolerance in discourse, except for the high value it places on the freedom of inquiry, a characteristic hardly unique to pragmatism. It is rather to expose a basic misunderstanding in the opposition to the tolerance of lies. That tolerance is not based on *any* assumption about the nature of the truth; it is, rather, founded on an assumption about the nature of the mind in its relation to the truth. I can believe (in fact I do, but that isn't the point here) that there is such a thing as absolute truth, that such a truth is beyond any determination by debate, beyond any relativism whatever, and *yet* believe that every individual mind must have the freedom to conduct just such a debate about the truth within itself, even about the truth of the Holocaust.

Whatever the problems with absolute intellectual tolerance—and there are many, so many that such a thing is not really possible in our world in any literal sense—they do not include any reliance upon a simplistic version of pragmatism, or upon a naive faith in fair play or in the capability of the mind always to see through falsehood to discern the truth. Whatever the problems with the Millian distinctions between the private and the public in convictions and behavior—and there are many, though Mill is a great deal more subtle than many of his detractors understand—his fundamental belief is sound, that "in each person's own concerns, his individual spontaneity is entitled to free exercise."[8] This is true, not because the truth will inevitably win out in the course of that free exercise, but because given the nature of human understanding, there is simply no viable alternative in a society which purports to base itself upon the independent judgment of the individual.

We can, of course, imagine a society in which the "truth" is dictated to its members. There are many actual models to choose from. What Noel seems to imagine is a society in which certain truths are, in effect, dictated to an otherwise-free constituency. Since these truths are, in fact, true, the majority would presumably not require such dictatorial persuasion, but there would still be a good many among the misguided, the recalcitrant, the pathological, the just plain evil, who would. This is, of course, exactly the way many of the most oppressive of the world's "people's republics" actually work; many kinds of "free speech" are permitted, but there are distinct regions of "truth" in which such speech is legally defined as seditious lies and punished accordingly.

My worthy opponent knows this very well; he can properly boast of an excellent track record of publishing the views of those who dare to test the boundaries of freedom in this particular republic. The problem is that, like all those before him who have sought to spread truth by denying a place to lies, he has failed to find satisfactory answers to the old questions, "who shall decide?" and "which truths are to be beyond debate?" It is simply not enough to say that a truth such as the death of six million Jews in the Holocaust is so compelling that anyone who does not accept it is, by some consensus of truth-tellers, denied the right to argue the point. That transforms a truth into a dogma. While it is obviously the case that we all take many things to be true on faith, or without seriously debating them within ourselves, it is quite another thing to be told that there are some things that we *must* take on faith, that we have no right to question. The independent imagination rebels at this, chafes even at being told not to question assertions it would otherwise not think to question. It seems clear to me that a good many of the young neo–Nazis, "Skinheads," and Holocaust-deniers are drawn to their folly by just this appeal to rebellion against authority.

I must confess that as a civil libertarian I do have faith that truth will — given enough time — prevail in the human imagination. The truth of the Holocaust, according to this faith, has no need of the force of dogma, even if such a thing would work. This, perhaps, makes me as naive as Noel charges, but in fact, even without such a faith, I see no alternative to giving the individual mind the freedom to grow, and to grasp, as it will.

There is danger in such freedom, it is true, and as I indicate above, the danger is such that absolute tolerance can never be regarded as more than a guiding ideal. The real differences between the advocacy position set forth by Noel and that of the civil libertarian are centered here in the area of freedom's dangerousness: To what degree is the marketplace, which we all agree is rigged, so hostile to the truth that it cannot make its way without special measures? Are the lies currently making their way in that marketplace so dangerous to the truth that special measures of intervention, special allocation of resources, are in order?

These are real questions which no civil libertarian can afford to dismiss. There are times when defending and advocating the truth does become a distinctly different activity, and of a higher priority, than providing access to all points of view. If one is air-dropping leaflets into an enemy country in wartime, it hardly seems appropriate to drop a "balanced collection" of enemy and friendly propaganda—and there are many in this country who feel, not without reason, that they are carrying messages to a hostile, or at least a captive, populace. One's sense of just how much freedom the marketplace of ideas allows will have a strong effect on the degree to which one is willing to play by its rules.

But we are librarians serving a people whose public ideal, laws, and most cherished documents—in particular, the First Article of the Bill of Rights—purport to place a good deal of confidence in the sorting powers of the marketplace of ideas. Thus there is a presumption, hardly unquestioned or unqualified, but nonetheless dominant, that access to the broadest range of ideas and information is conducive to the practice of democracy. This means that denying such access is an action that should be sharply questioned. And in this context, the question comes down to this: If David McCalden and his little band had been allowed exhibit space at the conference of the California Library Association, and if he had been allowed his meeting room and his little program that Sunday evening, would that act of tolerance toward a lie, a vicious and monumental lie, to be sure, have threatened the existence of the truth and the well-being of those who genuinely seek the truth? As I hope is clear by now, I think not, and only the most anxiety-ridden of those who fear the slippery slope to Hell would think otherwise.

This is not to say that I would therefore have let the man have his exhibit and his meeting. As I indicated in my original article, I too would probably have opted to save the Association rather than preserve a small and disputed corner of liberty. But that would have been—as it was, in fact—a political decision, an unfortunate but necessary choice of priorities. In spite of the outpouring of rage, disgust, hurt, and threats, political and otherwise, I would not have tried to convert my action of censorship into a high-minded gesture of distaste against someone who deserved no better. According to my understanding, both of the human spirit, and of the form of government which is, so far, the best incubator of that spirit, he — even he — did indeed deserve better.

References

1. Quoted by James M. O'Neill as an epigraph to his *Catholicism and American Freedom* (New York: Harper and Brothers, 1952).
2. Swan, "Untruth or Consequences," *Library Journal,* July 1986, p. 52.
3. In Levy, Leonard, *Emergence of a Free Press* (New York: Oxford University Press, 1985), p. 307. This superb history, an extensive revision of the author's *Legacy of Suppression* (and winner of the first American Library Association Eli Oboler Award), makes impossible any simplistic summary of the Founding Fathers' views of the practical implications of freedom of the press, and, not incidentally, should also render absurd any unified notion of a "jurisprudence of original intent."
4. Bok, Sissela, *Lying: Moral Choice in Public and Private Life* (New York: Vintage Books, 1979).
5. Bok, note, p. 311: "Is it deception or not? Intentional or not? Is there even communication or not? If a person appears to deceive himself, there are not two different human beings of whom one intends to deceive the other. Yet, arguably, two 'parts' of this person are involved in a deceptive relationship. Are there times when the right hand does not know what the left hand is doing? And times when the left hand is in fact deceiving the right hand? New research on brain function may show that there is then not so much a deceiver and a deceived, but rather two different processes coordinated by the brain...."
6. Peattie, Noel, "Cardinal Mazarin Is Dead?!" *Sipapu,* v. 17, no. 2, pp. 11-17.
7. Murphy, Arthur E., "The Pragmatic Theory of Truth" in *Belief, Knowledge, and Truth: Readings in the Theory of Knowledge,* ed. by Marcus Ammerman and Marcus Singer (New York: Scribner's, 1970), p. 443 (from Murphy's *The Uses of Reason,* 1943).
8. Mill, *On Liberty,* p. 94.

A Brief Rejoinder

Noel Peattie

John Swan's rebuttal to my paper is one of the best things he has written (and he has an extensive bibliography), but I couldn't help thinking that it should have been aimed at somebody else. At whom? No need to name names—some of the most insistent truth-tellers are among the best friends I have in the profession.

Swan's critique of my position may be taken for my argument's sake as making the following points: •I claim to be able to tell truth from lies, and truth-tellers from liars. •I wish to police the world, guide people to the truth, make them accept dogma, etc., and so forth. •I wish to appoint guardians who themselves will be un-guarded. •However, I am "fuzzy"—as apart from my cat, who is unquestionably furry. •I desire intervention in the marketplace of ideas. •I really am a libertarian (for this last, thank you). To all of these accusations, your petitioner "humbly sheweth":

No, I can't always tell truth from lies, nor truth-tellers from liars. The classic case, in which it has become almost impossible to tell one from the other, is the debate surrounding the assassination of President John F. Kennedy—a debate which has attained the status of an industry. I happen to have my own views on the subject, but I have misgivings about my own views, and am not really well informed on the whole business. What I do say, is that McCalden is a self-confessed racist (see reference number 8 on page 102) and that racism is based on a Big Lie, namely that certain races are superior to others. Whether McCalden is sincere, is beyond my powers to determine. By his own account, in a pamphlet which I have lost, he has made havoc in a number of organizations: in an anti-hunting league in Britain, in the American Atheists, and now among librarians. If he is sincere, he is a sincere trouble-maker. If he is not sincere, what is he?

No, I don't want to police the world. One of my sharpest critics has been my old friend Whitney H. Gordon, of Ball State University, who recently spent four months in Indonesia, and found the concepts advanced in an earlier version of my paper far too reminiscent of that country's "guided democracy." So I toned those comments down (thus becoming "fuzzy"), and placed my reliance on personal self-respect and collective honor.

I should point out, however, that both John Swan and I are far more policemen, guides, whatever you want to call the roles, than we possibly admit to ourselves. Both of us are white male Christian-heritage American professionals in the information business (he runs a small library, I work for a larger one, but also have my own newsletter). From the point of view of other groups — Jews protesting McCalden, blacks protesting ALA's film, *The speaker,* Muslims protesting Salman Rushdie — the Swans and Peatties of this world are indeed men of power. By tolerating these speakers, films, authors, we, at the center (as they see it) of world information, place ourselves on the side of their enemies. Call it paranoid, call it intolerant, but the view of the "outsiders" has a certain point. I have little sympathy for the "New World Information Order" that gained some attention a few years ago, largely because it reminded me of Hitler's "New World Order" — but I could see its sponsors' point, that Western reporting on the Third World is either trivial, or focuses on disasters, dictatorships, debts and deforestation. Real progress gets shunted to page 32.

In that case we *are* guardians, and we *are* unguarded. I certainly am in no position to tell John Swan how to run Bennington College Library: but I can appeal to all of us to mind our consciences. (I am sure he does).

If, then, we criticize the people who proposed to picket the hotel where McCalden was to speak, we are really "blaming the victims." This point is brought out at several places in Gill Seidel's book,* which I only discovered after I had written "Truth, libraries, and revolution." Her book makes my points about freedom of

---

Gill Seidel, The Holocaust denial: antisemitism, racism, and the New Right *(London, Beyond the Pale Collective, distributed by Turnaround Books, 1986).*

expression, falsehood in history, and the imbalance of power, far better than I can.

What Seidel shows is that the "Holocaust revisionists" are part of a large network, and that dealings with them should be understood and handled accordingly. If in the marketplace of ideas, which Swan and I agree is subtly controlled, it is deemed necessary to have their books or admit their speakers, then Swan's idea of "more speech" should apply. Seidel's book should be on the shelf, and she should be invited to speak along with McCalden. As it happens, I don't recall having seen Seidel's book reviewed — perhaps because it is from a small radical publisher — and I only found it by looking under the appropriate subject heading in our on-line catalog.

I really am a libertarian. Thank you! And so is anyone who finds his identity threatened, and therefore his liberty. If McCalden wants free speech, then I want to be able to say, "Aw, shaddup!" without being lectured to by libertarians.

Finally, I find no demonstration by Swan of the contrary of my thesis: that a society in which the dignity of the oppressed is respected is ultimately more free than a society in which they are insulted or injured. Nor do I see contradicted my thesis that our intellectual defenses are weak in dealing with neo-Nazis. In those regards, I fear our work is yet to be done.

Three Hard Cases for Socially Responsible Librarians (An Appendix)

Noel Peattie

Of the innumerable cases which have confronted librarians who have made some sort of a commitment to social responsibility or social consciousness, however vaguely defined, I select three recent problems, without any expectation that any answer, other than a glib one, can be given which will leave the social-responsibility sector, or any sector of opinion in Libraryland, entirely happy. I adduce these problems as examples of the general truth, that no position taken in this debate is without its drawbacks.

No. 1

In 1981 the Forsyth County Library in Winston-Salem, North Carolina, allowed the Invisible Empire of the **Ku Klux Klan to use its library meeting space,** in spite of threats of violence, and in spite of earlier experiences of violence on the occasion of the showing of a KKK exhibit.[1] The Library had previously opened its auditorium to groups generally perceived as "left," such as the Committee Against Registration and the Draft, and the Committee in Solidarity with the People of El Salvador. The vote was taken, after five months of deliberation, by the Forsyth County Commissioners.

The citation mentions a "model meeting room policy," which may have been modeled on, or derived from, the *Library Bill of Rights* (53.1.6): "Libraries which make exhibit space and meeting rooms available to the public they serve should make such facilities available on an equitable basis, regardless of the beliefs or affiliations of individuals or groups requesting their use."[2]

Further interpretation (ALA *Policy manual,* 53.1.8) brings us to the following: "Libraries maintaining exhibit and meeting room facilities should develop and publish statements governing their use. These statements can properly define and restrict eligibility for use as long as the qualifications do not pertain to the content of a meeting or exhibit or to the beliefs or affiliations of the sponsors, and are applied on an equitable basis."[3]

Assuming that the Forsyth County Library may have the *Library Bill of Rights* publicly posted, or in some other way let the public know of its existence; or that its model meeting room policy incorporates the language or (at least) the spirit of these two passages, it would be hard for the library to avoid opening the auditorium to the Ku Klux Klan. The Library had opened its meeting room doors to organizations on the other end of the political spectrum. The fact that the Library might be picketed by the Klan's opponents, and that a violent confrontation might have taken place (as had happened in nearby Greensboro) was a good reason for delaying the decision on the Klan's application to use the meeting room. But, as in the McCalden case, where violence was also threatened when a racist was given a chance to speak, the threat of violence was not the philosophical point at issue.

In this case Swan and I are surely on the same side; given the policy of the Forsyth County Library, which I presume was publicly known, the Library could not weasel out of its commitment to equality. The most that a socially conscious librarian could do in these potentially explosive circumstances would be to notify the Federal Bureau of Investigation to be alert for any trouble. However, if the FBI offered to "bug" the room, the librarian would have to say no. To "bug" a room is to discriminate against the people using it, and that the Library has already pledged not to do. In such a situation the librarian would be standing between an organization known to have been involved in violent actions in the past, and a major law-enforcement agency of the Federal government. The ethical complications of this scenario are troubling to contemplate.

No. 2

The second problem I select for study, is the collision of traditional First Amendment supporters with the new **feminist opponents of pornography,** and the counter-move by some women who, notwithstanding their dislike of pornography, oppose legal sanctions to remove it.[4]

The traditional position of librarians defending the First Amendment from censors has been that obscenity, pornography, and erotica, however defined or left undefined, frequently confused and used interchangeably, were purely subjective terms. They existed only in the reader's mind; one reader's erotica was another reader's pornography, and once a book or periodical had been acquired, it was the librarian's duty to defend it—indeed the duty of all librarians to rush to any one librarian's defense when beleaguered by the citizenry for acquiring it. No reader, librarians announced, had the right to deny another reader the chance to read a book, regardless of the words in it or the actions described or depicted in it. The object of this stance was to defend the inclusion, in library collections, of the works of Henry Miller, D.H. Lawrence, and other authors of the early modern period.[5]

At the same time, librarians exercised due caution with sexually explicit materials where local pressure was strongly against them—which was likely to be anywhere; and librarians left the so-called "adult bookstores" to pick up the most explicit material. Such bookstores are, however, only a development of the past twenty years, a period in which (partly thanks to the liberal decisions of the courts that Rembar describes) books and periodicals have become far more sexually explicit than they were thirty years ago. In addition, "soft porn," defined as nonviolent sexually explicit material, was followed by "hard-core porn," which includes scenes depicting the torture, mutilation, and deaths of women. Against this depiction of atrocities, feminists protested, and on the ground that the depiction was likely to influence men to go out and perform the acts depicted: "pornography is the theory, rape is the practice." (Note that this presents an entirely different set of reactions from that involved in the McCalden case; nobody has ever suggested that hearing McCalden, or indeed reading about the Holocaust, will inspire librarians or anyone else, to go out and kill Jews.)

An essential (and perhaps the first) book in this field is *Take back the night.*[6] It consists of essays by different authors on the dangers of pornography to women, studies showing the effect of pornography on men, and discussions of the work of the various Federal commissions that have investigated the problem.

Gloria Steinem, in her essay in that book, "Erotica and pornography: a clear and present difference," makes the distinction between sexuality and power: "Perhaps one could simply say that erotica is about sexuality, but pornography is about power and sex-as-weapon" (p. 38).

The legal question of pornography is in the book's Section V. Wendy Kaminer's essay, "Pornography and the First Amendment: prior restraints and private action," takes the view that going to law is not the solution: "We simply cannot look to the government to rid us of pornography; legally there can be no 'final solutions.' The feminist movement against pornography must remain an anti-defamation movement involved in education, consciousness-raising, and the development of private strategies against the industry" (p. 247).

Robin Yeamans gives us "A political-legal analysis of pornography"; she notes that the Supreme Court changed its mind over segregation; it "can and must be convinced in the pornography area" (p. 250). She sees pornography as "speech soliciting people to commit crimes" and foresees a future in which the rights of media owners give way before the rights of battered women and children.

The essay in *Take back the night,* "Let's put pornography back in the closet," by Susan Brownmiller, makes the "distinction between permission to publish and permission to display publicly," which to my mind is hopelessly vague. "For men, freedom of speech; for women, silence please," by Andrea Dworkin, takes the view that men have all the power and that the First Amendment really belongs to them. "The First Amendment . . . belongs to those who can buy it" (p. 258). She wants lawyers to make the Amendment work for women, without giving any clear details as to how this might be applied.

This last view is echoed by Ruthann Robson, who examines the tensions between male freedom and the censorship of women, finally coming down on the side of social pressure instead of legal sanctions: "We must silence pornography — by speaking up louder and louder and over and over. We cannot expect laws to do that which should be done by persons. Public opinion has always been the best censor."[7]

In her interview in *Sipapu,* Lily Pond, editor of *Yellow silk; journal of erotic arts,* says, "Anything that censors anything will censor *Yellow Silk,* which is why I'm against any kind of censorship of sexual pornography. And I said it before and I'll say it again: the only way to combat it is to create a strong, healthy alternative — which is what I'm doing."[8] She goes on to make the distinction between those who create because it is "within the artist's heart," and those who write or draw pornography just to make money.

The symposium *Perspectives on pornography,* published in 1970, included thirteen men and one woman. This immediately dates it, of course, but the book does include antipornography writers, as well as those in favor of it.[9] It is with the woman's essay that I will be concerned with here, since the author is a well-known philosopher.[10]

Susan Sontag focuses on pornography as a "minor but highly interesting modality or convention within the arts,"[11] and examines contemporary French literature, notably Georges Bataille's *Histoire de l'Oeil, Histoire d'O* signed by "Pauline Réage," and *L'Image* signed by "Jean de Berg." Works by Sade, Genet, and other works by Bataille are also cited. For Sontag, these are explorations into the loss of the self, the darker side of eroticism, which English and American critics fail to appreciate. The descriptions Sontag gives of these books make them terrifying, surrealistic; it would be impossible for me to get any pleasure out of a book like *Story of O:* "Her achievement is represented in the last scene of the book when she's led to a party, mutilated, in chains, unrecognizable, costumed (as an owl) — so convincingly no longer human that none of the guests even thinks of speaking to her directly."[12]

Although this seems to be the antithesis of the consciousness of modern feminist sensibility, so that I am amazed that a woman can find anything to admire in such a book, still Sontag has a deeper insight than Robson. Robson says: "Andrea Dworkin, in her recent book, *Pornography: Men Possessing Women,* agrees that pornography is properly defined as 'the graphic depiction of whores.'"[13] But according to Sontag, "Bataille understood more clearly than anyone else that what pornography is really about, ultimately, isn't sex, but death."[14]

Sontag does indeed share the sense of distress others share concerning the availability of cheap pornography, but concludes that it is not knowledge, including knowledge of the darker sides of eroticism, that poses the danger, but the abuse of knowledge. If we really want to protect society from itself we should have to do more censoring than just that which is applied to the pornographic: all serious forms of art and knowledge are dangerous.

The most extensive account of the movement of women against censorship of pornographic or erotic works comes from a Canadian viewpoint. *Women against censorship*[15] includes a number of reasons why, although pornography is degrading and may even be dangerous, some women wish to avoid making it illegal. For Varda Burstyn, the antipornography movement brings the feminist movement into alliance with conservatives and plays into the hands of a patriarchal society. For Myrna Kostash, pornographic images are so prevalent, and fantasies so plainly common to both sexes, that any attempt to censor pornography would censor both the (harmless) erotic and the (dangerous) pornographic — probably the first before the second. For Sara Diamond, the answer to the pornography problem is to create positive visions of women's sexuality, including lesbian sexuality. For Lisa Steele, advertising is the real enemy; it reinforces sexist messages to a wide variety of people who never enter an "adult bookstore." For Lynn King, whose essay is titled "Censorship and law reform: will changing the laws make a change for the better?" the answer is *no*. She points out that once installed in office, the censor must have something to do; and the more he censors (the pronoun is intentional), the more he can justify his paycheck. For Anna Gronau, who was a programmer for films at The Funnel, a Toronto theatre for experimental film, the Ontario Board of Censors censored exactly the kind of liberating film that the women at The Funnel wanted to promote. . .

In short, the remedy, as typified by excerpts from a Minneapolis ordinance against pornography, quoted at the end of *Women against censorship,* is worse than the disease. I remember the conversation I had with Betty-Carol Sellen of Brooklyn College Library, coauthor (though I did not know it then) of the major bibliography cited in note 4: I had said that I didn't like pornography, but that I was opposed to outlawing it. Sellen looked at me narrowly. The following colloquy ensued:

N.P. "Let me ask you two questions. Do you believe that there is a difference between erotica and pornography?" B.-C.S. (reluctantly) "Yes." N.P. "Then tell me: have you ever heard a pompous Fourth of July orator intone, 'Ours is a government of laws, and not of men'?" B.-C.S. (Grim smile).

This is, of course, the position taken by King and Gronau in this book from Canada. Enough of this review of the literature: enough to show that among women — whose voices on this matter have long been ignored or suppressed — there is a considerable spectrum of opinion. The question "pornography/erotica — yes or no?" is, however, not answered in the terms that male civil libertarians answer it in; "freedom for what we want means freedom for the detestable" does not turn up in the essays I have explored. In *Women against censorship,* there is instead a strong emphasis on female values and a deep suspicion of a male-dominated government. In Sontag's essay there is a clear emphasis on stereotype, ritual, artifice: she and other essayists compare pornography with science fiction. She also describes the pornographic literature of the eighteenth century, with its debauched noblemen who hold women captive in impossible castles: an artifice revived in some of her contemporary favorites. John Fowles's novel, *The collector,* and its successor, *The magus,* rely on the same convention: the terrible house from which one cannot escape (though neither book is remotely pornographic).

And this brings us back to the Holocaust. What was Europe from 1942 to 1945 — from the Wannsee Conference to V-E Day, but a huge house of horror from which millions of Jews and others could not escape, presided over by a deformed artist, a terrible magus? I suggest that Sontag's statement, that pornography is really about death, would be best appreciated by none other than Hitler himself.

If Susan Sontag finds value in the terrifying fictions of Georges Bataille, should she be asked to speak at a library conference? Wouldn't she be seen, at least by some librarians there, as promoting a lie different in some ways, but similar in others, to the one McCalden was perceived as promoting?

Is hard porn a lie? A picture of a naked body is not a lie; a picture of a tortured body is not a lie. Otherwise we would have to dismiss Goya's *Disasters of war,* and much of the work of Callot. But many people tell us that pornography tells lies about women. In the case of commercial depiction of nakedness in *Playboy* or in advertising, the trouble is not in the bodies themselves but in the spirit that the maker of the image has brought to its making. The judgment of Lily Pond, that it is the heart of the artist which matters, seems to me to be, if not irrefutable, at least central to any discussion of the issue of pornography, and her emphasis on a healthy alternative, which is also shared by Diamond in *Women against censorship,* is the most useful. However, I still don't know what would happen if Susan Sontag were to read aloud from Bataille's novels at a library conference.

When it comes to human reactions, to scenes of violence and sexuality, then our information is scanty and conflicting. Tests of reactions to erotica or pornography are difficult to make and usually can only involve a limited number of people; while mass audiences react to television, the samples are usually small. And the only way to test people's reactions to the violence of war would be to start one, and then question the survivors — which is morally (though not practically) out of the question.

As regards individuals, studies of them are not much help either, as everyone's autobiography has elements of the unique. I used to like the pictures in *Playboy:* now I don't. Does this mean I am more socially conscious, more responsible, or does it illustrate the remark attributed to Sir Charles Sherrington in one of his medical lectures: "Gentlemen, we know only two things about the brain; one, that it likes the same stimulus; two, that it doesn't"?

The truth about pornography seems to be this: we don't know what it is, we don't know what it does to people's minds (or rather, it seems to please some and displease others, and that it is apparent *here,* but not [or maybe also] over *there*); and consequently nobody knows what to do about it. Everyone is entitled to his or her private fantasies, but what constitutes a safe release of them, is yet to be agreed upon. Many are able to tolerate a little of it, but few want an adult bookstore on their block. A fresh approach, although a specialized one, is given by Alex Comfort: "*pornography* — Name given to any sexual literature somebody is trying to suppress."[16]

Here again, there is no clear dichotomy between truth and freedom, access and atmosphere. Kostash, and Robson, agree on describing ours as a pornographic society, but both agree that it is women's real sexuality, and their frank expression of it, which is suppressed first — and then both draw back when someone raises the possibility of censorship. "All feel the Ill, yet shun the Cure:/ Can Sense this Paradox endure?"[17]

As long as Prior's diagnosis holds true for the pornographic society, there can be no easy answers, for writers, speakers, readers or librarians. As I compared Truth to the currency, let me compare pornography to mustard: it tastes great on sausages, but nobody wants a whole meal of it.

No. 3

A third problem for American librarians arises out of the proposed **cultural boycott of the Republic of South Africa.** The nature of the apartheid regime is familiar to all. Pseudoindependent states, such as Transkei, totally dependent on South Africa, have been set up as puppet regimes within the white-controlled Republic. Foreign powers, including the United States and Britain, have taken an ambiguous, wavering course toward the racist regime in Pretoria. Sanctions and disinvestment from these countries have been unevenly applied: they are not complete, nor are they likely to be.

The African National Congress, the largest opposition party in the Republic of South Africa, suffers from several disadvantages in its campaign to acquire national liberation. It lacks a standing army, aircraft and artillery, a territorial base, an industrial plant; having renounced nonviolence some years ago, it finds its guerrillas promptly attacked and arrested, and its bases on foreign soil are often attacked by South African commando raids. The Pan African Congress, a militant splinter group, commands an even smaller loyalty and is equally powerless to overthrow its white racist enemy. The only hope of liberation movements in South Africa is to induce elements of a liberal persuasion in the West to boycott South African products and to impose sanctions on white-ruled South Africa.[18]

The amount of disengagement advocated by those who see such disengagement as the way to end apartheid has been variously reported; the literature is voluminous, but it is not always accurate. David Beaty and Oren Harari[19] summarize the arguments concerning disengagement, pro and con. On the basis of two years' research in South Africa, they conclude that disinvestment is likely to have only a trivial effect on the total South African economy. American-owned firms operating in South Africa employ only 1 percent of the total black work force. The likelihood of the white population's abandoning apartheid, to which they have a strong emotional and even religious attachment, is zero. The authors state that a black takeover of South Africa is inevitable: which seems strange in view of their assertion that the white control is effective and absolute. They speak of "the immense blanketlike white military and police apparatus that is at the disposal of the South African government."[20]

Concerning arguments for and against disinvestment, Beaty and Harari find both sides weak on logic and slow to recognize the grim realities of life and work in South Africa today. Firms which operate in South Africa, endeavoring to liberalize conditions by integrating the shop floor, come in for criticisms from blacks who force their white employers to realize that once the black workers leave the factory gates, they are second-class citizens in a police state. The very idea of "help" has a different meaning for whites and for blacks; the "good" employer, for black South Africans, is the employer who pays an activist employee his wages even when that employee is in jail (which can be a long time). The black voice, therefore, calls upon the foreign employer to make some effort to change the society in South Africa *in general,* instead of merely extending privileges to a few workers.

Given these conditions, Beaty and Harari find disengagement on the part of American and other foreign firms and groups as largely symbolic and moral, and not necessarily effective save in the very long run. Moral and symbolic actions are not powerless or trivial — witness the attention paid to flags in all nations or nations coming-to-be, or temporarily eclipsed — but neither are they as immediately effective as (for example) an armored division. This leads right into the question of cultural disengagement, and where it takes us in Libraryland.

The earliest responses of the library community to the disengagement challenge were in the form of disinvestment of the American Library Association's funds. In June 1985, the American Library Association Council, with the endorsement of the membership, directed ALA's endowment trustees to divest ALA's stock portfolio of corporations doing business in South Africa.[21] Efforts to challenge South African apartheid on a personal level were initiated when past ALA President E.J. Josey rose at the Chicago conference of the International Federation of Library Associations to protest the presence of twelve South African delegates (all of whom were white). A subsequent resolution barred from IFLA membership those South African libraries that continued to practice apartheid.[22]

In 1986 Congress passed, and the president signed into law, the Comprehensive Anti-Apartheid Act, which restricted trade in a number of items with South Africa. In the wake of this law, a number of cities required major vendors doing business with the city to show that they did no business with South Africa. San Francisco and Chicago warned the book wholesalers Baker & Taylor that their libraries would have to change jobbers unless Baker & Taylor's parent company, W.R. Grace & Co., pulled their plants out of South Africa.[23] Houston, whose library obtains materials from Britain's Library Association, got a stinging rebuttal when they sent a compliance form to London to be filled out, and the Houston City Council subsequently exempted the Houston Public Library from the city ordinance.[24] In 1988 a bill to strengthen the original Anti-Apartheid Act was introduced into the House, which exempted books and periodicals from the list of materials prevented from reaching South Africa. A similar bill was introduced into the Senate, and was reported out by the Foreign Relations Committee, but the threat of a filibuster and of a presidential veto, as well as protests from the British Embassy concerning the fate of offshore oil leases, prevented it from being debated on the Senate floor.[25]

Some publishers, included in Houston's ban on trading with South Africa, declined to ship books thereto,[26] but the Association of American Publishers took the stand that the free flow of information would do more to end apartheid than curtailment would, and refused to join the boycott.[27] In view of the restrictions on information in South Africa, where advocating disinvestment is a serious crime, and where bigoted attitudes are justified by an appeal to Scripture, this view seems naive.[28] In any case, few of the American volumes would be likely to reach black libraries; at best, they might reach a few well-disposed whites.[29]

At the 1986 annual conference of the American Library Association in New York, the membership opposed the entry of the South African Institute of Librarianship and Information Science (SAILIS) into IFLA until SAILIS takes a strong stand on open membership and equal education, and toes the line on a number of other points.[30] This action provoked a strong reaction from the president of SAILIS, Anna Louw, who charged that SAILIS had already opened its membership (18 September 1986), and who further charged that ALA seemed to have a strong prejudice against the professional librarians of South Africa.[31]

The next American Library Association annual conference met in San Francisco, where the intellectual freedom forces once again clashed with the social responsibilities crowd: "A controversial resolution putting ALA in opposition to government restrictions on trade [in ideas and information] with South Africa was defeated by the members, but not until bitter debate between the motion's sponsor, Dorothy Broderick, and former ALA president E.J. Josey."[32] The Executive Board of the Intellectual Freedom Round Table had apparently decided to press the resolution, allegedly on the ground that a certain library was unable to maintain, under local rules, a subscription to *The Wall Street journal* because the *Journal* has a correspondent in South Africa. The opposition to the resolution was based on the fact that it would have undermined ALA's position on apartheid, which stems from the concerns of the resolutions passed at the 1986 conference, and also on ALA *Policy manual* 57.3: "Abridgement of the rights of freedom of foreign nationals." ALA's "Current Reference File" has a paper on "Abridgement of human rights in South Africa."[33]

The African Studies Association witnessed a debate in the form of conflicting papers by Ismail Abdullahi, a student of E.J. Josey's, who urged a comprehensive academic and informational boycott of South Africa, and Lorraine Haricombe, a black South African librarian studying at the University of Illinois, who argued that such denial of information hurt those whom it was trying to help.[34]

Amid all these marches and counter-marches, Beaty and Harari would doubtless perceive a lack in the business community to which they addressed their paper: a lack of input from black South African librarians themselves. With the exception of Haricombe, none of the speakers or corporate bodies seem to have done much listening to the people they were talking about. Beaty and Harari stress in their paper the concept of "naive listening," which they describe as "Americans going *to* black South Africans, sitting down with them on their turf and in their language, and *really* listening to them on their terms without arguing or even responding" (Beaty and Harari, p. 43). Rejecting "bandying about survey data" and urging that Americans "keep mouths shut and ears open," the authors conclude that 49 percent of black South Africans endorse "conditional disinvestment" (which means, Americans, help us change the system or get out) while 24 percent support *total* disinvestment, with 26 percent supporting current United States policy (p. 44). A survey derived from a large sample (their error was no more than 4 percent) of black South African librarians might come up with some interesting results. Unfortunately Dr. Harari is back in the United States, and Dr. Beaty, whose article might have placed him in jeopardy for seeming to advocate disinvestment, has accepted employment here and is also living somewhere in the United States.

Others who wish to visit South Africa may be easily misled,

or coopted, while being attacked by those who hold that any visit to the Republic supports the racist regime. In any case, it looks as if anyone who goes there, certainly any white person, will find himself in a hall of mirrors which it is in the interest of the government and most of its white population to set up.[35]

Once again, truth is prior to freedom: we must know the truth, have "one eye cocked" on it, before we can act freely; and once again, it pays to sit down and "listen naively" to what Jews, women, and black South Africans really have to say, before holding forth with the noble words of Jefferson or Mill.

In the absence of such a survey or any collective statement by black South African librarians and readers themselves — which statement is not to be expected, since speaking out in favor of disinvestment carries a heavy fine and lengthy jail sentence, socially responsible librarians are in a difficult position. It would probably be counterproductive, and it certainly would arouse the ire of the faculty, if an American university library were to cancel its subscription to a South African scientific or medical journal. On the other hand, libraries can certainly balance their collections with materials from organizations working against apartheid, and a list of these organizations has been compiled by the South Africa Information Project, College of Library and Information Services, University of Maryland.[36] Accepting that almost anything done here in the United States will be largely ethical and symbolic, and that no real profound change can be expected in South Africa in the near future (according to Parliament member Helen Sulzman), librarians can nevertheless continue their traditional devotion to freedom of information by gathering information as close to the real source as humanly possible. The South African situation is intractable; but we can at least arm ourselves with the *facts*.[37]

References

1. *Library journal,* v. 106, no. 11, p. 1156 (June 1, 1981).
2. American Library Association *Handbook of organization,* p. 241.
3. *Ibid.*
4. The literature is voluminous. See: Betty-Carol Sellen and Patricia A. Young, *Feminists, pornography and the law: an annotated bibliography of conflict, 1970–1986* (Hamden, Conn., Shoe String Press, Library Professional Publications, 1987); Greg Byerly, *Pornography: the conflict over sexually explicit materials in the United States* (New York, Garland, 1980); *Perspectives on pornography,* edited with an introduction by Douglas A. Hughes (New York, St.

Martin's Press, 1970); Ruthann Robson, "Pornography, power, and the First Amendment" (*New Pages: news and reviews of the progressive book trade,* v. 2, no. 1 [spring 1982], p. 9–13 [reprinted in *Alternative library literature, 1982–1983*<Phoenix, Oryx Press, 1984>, p. 68–75]).
5. An account of this period in the history of publishing will be found in Charles Rembar, *The end of obscenity: the trials of Lady Chatterley, Tropic of Cancer, and Fanny Hill* (New York, Random House, 1968).
6. *Take back the night: women on pornography,* edited by Laura Lederer (New York, Morrow, 1980).
7. Ruthann Robson, "Pornography, power, and the First Amendment," *New Pages,* op. cit., p. 75.
8. *Sipapu,* v. 16, no. 1 (consec. no. 31), p. 12.
9. *Perspectives on pornography,* edited with an introduction by Douglas A. Hughes (New York, St. Martin's Press, 1970).
10. Susan Sontag, "The pornographic imagination," *Perspectives on pornography,* [131]–169.
11. *Ibid.,* p. [131].
12. *Ibid.,* p. 152.
13. Robson, op. cit., p. 69.
14. *Perspectives on pornography,* p. 156–157.
15. *Women against censorship,* edited by Varda Burstyn (Vancouver, Douglas & McIntyre, 1985).
16. Alex Comfort, ed., *The joy of sex: a cordon bleu guide to lovemaking* (New York, Simon and Schuster, 1972), p. 208–209. The whole short essay, only four paragraphs, is typical of the candor, but also the limitations, of Alex Comfort's comforting books.
17. Matthew Prior, "Written in the beginning of Mezeray's History of France."
18. A full bibliography on the sanctions and disinvestment movement does not seem to exist. For background, see the coverage (to 1980) from a radical perspective in *Africa today* (London, Africa Journal Ltd., 1980). *Africa contemporary record, annual survey and documents* (New York, Africana Publishing Co., 1968–69–   ), has an extensive coverage (in its 1978–1979 volume) of "The Southern African crisis, 1986–1987" (p. A3–A–79); "The SDACC on the front line" (p. A80–A97); and "South Africa" (p. B717–B830). The African National Congress's position on sanctions is briefly described by two quotes on p. B765.
19. David Beaty and Oren Harari, "Divestment and disinvestment from South Africa: a reappraisal," *California management review,* v. 29, no. 4, summer 1987, p. 31–40.
20. *Ibid.,* p. 39.
21. See, e.g., Milo Nelson, "Fifty ways to leave your lover," *Wilson library bulletin,* 60:4, December 1985, p. 4.
22. "Sleep no more at IFLA," *American libraries,* October 1985, p. 610, 612, 614.
23. "Grace South African plants may cost Baker & Taylor," *American libraries,* November 1986, p. 741–742; "Libraries warn Baker & Taylor on ties to South Africa," *Publishers weekly,* October 3, 1986, p. 29.
24. "British L.A. rebuffs Houston's S. Africa boycott," *American libraries,* June 1987, p. 408–409; "Houston exempts library from South Africa ban," *American libraries,* December 1987, p. 889.
25. "House votes to exclude publishers from South Africa trading ban," *Publishers weekly,* September 2, 1988, p. 16; "Senate bill would free books from new limits on South Africa exports," *Publishers weekly,* September 23, 1988, p. 12. See also *CQ weekly reports,* October 29, 1988, p. 3129.
26. Gloria Miklowitz, "Why deny the children?" *Publishers weekly,* October 9, 1987, p. 66.

27. "AAP Board votes to reject South Africa book boycott," *Publishers weekly,* January 29, 1988, p. 312.
28. See Beaty and Harari, p. 39, 41.
29. Mokumbung Nkomo, "The South African library system — unequal funding, unequal service," *Interracial books for children bulletin,* v. 16, nos. 5/6, 1985 (reprinted in *Alternative library literature, 1984–1985* [Jefferson, N.C., McFarland, 1985], p. 205–206).
30. *American libraries,* July/August 1986, p. 520.
31. "Head of South African library group disputes ALA view," *American libraries,* April 1987, p. 243.
32. *Library journal,* August 1987, p. 25.
33. American Library Association *Handbook of organization, 1987–1988,* p. 246.
34. Helen MacLam, "South Africa and the free flow of information," *College and research libraries news,* v. 49, no. 11 (December 1988), p. 734–735.
35. Anthony Olden, "Should we visit South Africa?" *American libraries,* December 1988, p. 1001–1002. (A box in the article gives the views of Lorraine Haricombe, who is said to favor visits from international colleagues and exchange programs for librarians who serve black communities. Presumably this would emphasize black-on-black contact.) Replies to Olden's paper, pro and con, may be found in *American libraries,* February 1989, p. 122–123.
36. "Anti-apartheid resource guide," *Alternative library literature, 1984–1985,* p. 212–218.
37. E.J. Josey has called my attention to an article by Christopher Merrett, "Librarians in a police state: South African academic libraries and the problem of censorship," *Journal of librarianship.* 20:3 (July 1988), p. 181–193. Merrett, a British librarian working in South Africa, discusses the enormous range of censorship there in detail, sympathizes with the librarian as victim and faults him as collaborator, and charges the South African profession with timidity and inability to speak out against the apartheid system.

Two Last Socially Conscious Questions for Hardy Librarians (An Appendix)

John Swan

This morning a student came to me with a small pamphlet that he had found on the current periodical shelves. The title of the document is "Trial by Jewry," and it is essentially a comic book presentation of a point of view which this student and, I assume, most of the rest of us find abhorrent. It is a defense of one Ernst Zündel, a German-born Canadian who has been active in challenging the "lie" of the Holocaust and who was, after considerable legal struggle, sentenced to jail and deportation for his pains. "Canada has lost much of her freedom in recent years," the booklet tells us, "because of strategic pressure applied by special-interest groups, in particular a shrill minority of Jewish Zionists." Most of the crudely drawn panels are devoted to testimony and "evidence" from "experts" that there were no gas chambers, no death camps, no orders for a Final Solution. The final panel depicts "Boobus Northamericanus" with his finger in his mouth, saying, "I know the Holycaust [sic] happened 'cause I saw it on TV!"

Who published this little treatise? None other than our old acquaintance, the Truth Missions. Who placed it on our shelves? Perhaps the same person or persons who several months ago slipped many copies of another document into the books in our Holocaust collection, a widely disseminated single sheet bearing "66 Questions on the Holocaust" ("What extensive measure did world Jewry

undertake against Germany as early as 1933?" "Did the Jews of the
World 'declare war on Germany'?" "How does the 'Holocaust' story
benefit the Jews today? ... Christian clergymen? ... the communists?") published by that other familiar (and closely related) organization, the Institute for Historical Review. The student who found
"Trial by Jewry" was upset by its presence in our library, and I
shared his sense of violation. I could even sympathize with the student who found the "66 Questions" and brought me a copy with a
note saying someone had put it into many books: "I know it would
be hard to find out who it was, but could I suggest public hanging?"
And yes, in both cases we swiftly removed the offensive material
from the shelves.

Question Number One, then, suggests itself: If I claim to
tolerate the presence of such odious matter in the arena of public
discourse, why do I suppress it just as quickly as — I presume — Noel
Peattie would? In other words, is my First Amendment sunshine
argument just moonshine? As I have admitted in several places
earlier in this volume, there are countless practical limits upon the
tolerance of the lunatic fringe, dangerous or otherwise. The first and
most obvious answer to the question above is that *nothing* gets
slipped into the library's books or onto its shelves without professional screening, and the same fate would befall *The New York
Times* if it sneaked into our library without scrutiny before the acquisitions decision.

This, however, is begging the real question, and without going
again over the practical arguments, I shall hazard one more pass at
the direct question, as recast: Just *where* would I allow these
ideologies of hatred in the library? Part of the answer is simple: On
the shelves, once there is an acknowledged curricular need for it, or
a more general demand that is large enough to warrant the use of
the resources. If someone asked to see a copy of "Trial by Jewry,"
we'd endeavor to connect the patron with one, whether that person
were a scholar of social pathologies or an example of one. The rest
of the answer is not simple, is in fact rooted in considerations of cir-
cumstance and, for me, intimately involved in the answer to Question Number Two: Just how do we carry on trade in bad goods in
the Marketplace of Ideas? or, If no idea is to be expelled from said
market on grounds of mere despicableness, just how, and when, do
we devote what resources to such ideas?

As with Question Number One, part of the answer is simple, in
statement, if not in practice: We devote to them whatever the market

will bear. And this answer should bear some explication. Without rehearsing, once again, our collective problems with the very notion of said Marketplace of Ideas, I want to assert one more as-yet-unasserted vital fact about it: It is not, in fact, one market, but a multitude, with more-or-less fluid boundaries between them. For the most part, they share a single dynamic; that is, the ideas which one marketplace tests and finds "universal," it tends to attempt to export, as indeed universal, to all the other marketplaces.

For example, in one particular mart, the idea that Islam has been unacceptably blasphemed by the novel *The Satanic Verses,* and therefore its author should be killed, has so successfully won its way that it has become a matter of urgency that all other markets, and particularly the one in which its author lives and works, adopt the same idea. Although these are very different spheres, there is a great deal of fluidity in their boundaries, and Salman Rushdie had heretofore found wide success in both of them (his previous novels were best-sellers in Iran as well as India). The idea that he and his book ought to die is — very fortunately — anathema in the larger marketplace (or concatenation of marts) as decidedly as it is gospel in the other. However, a number of the inhabitants of the former have been convinced, or scared, into scolding the threatened author for (to quote one of them) "insensitively degrading and devaluing what millions of believing Muslims continue to perceive as sacrosanct."[1]

For many of us the argument is unacceptable that a creator — particularly one whose metier is the modern world of doubt and ambiguity forged in the clash of different cultures — ought to write as though a special set of beliefs, so obviously caught up in that clash, is "sacrosanct." But my belief that this editorialist is thoroughly in error when he accuses Rushdie of "calculated and senseless ridicule" is as conditioned by my own commitment to that marketplace of modernist doubt as his view is formed by his involvement, as a Princeton doctoral candidate in Islamic history, in that other marketplace. He agrees that "in our world Salman Rushdie has a right to do what he has done" that ought to be defended, and to this extent at least, we share one marketplace's assumptions and reject another's.

The point of all this is that the above answer to Question Number Two, "Whatever the marketplace will bear," has both its relativist and absolutist sides, and in practice both must be observed. One marketplace "bears" the idea that Rushdie should die (or at least be censored — even that sphere is anything but monolithic), the other does not, and the friction produces a number of very different, often mutually exclusive, ideas which compete in both markets, or many markets, freely and surreptitiously, openly and implicitly. The market grounded in principles of intellectual freedom tolerates all of these ideas — as ideas, not as actions — but while granting space to various criticisms of Rushdie, quickly rejected the notion that he should die, and almost as quickly established a broad consensus that the book should be allowed to roam free. Indeed, if the Ayatollah had uttered his death fiat as a British subject, he would very likely have found himself censored, perhaps indicted, a serious death threat being generally regarded as in the nature of shouting "Fire!" in a crowded theater. There is, in short, broad tolerance, and there are limits.

Those committed to the practice of intellectual freedom therefore are committed to a paradox, one which has been expressed in many ways, but which ought now be cast in the terms of the above (more or less tenable) metaphor: We grant the essential relativity of ideas as they are nurtured in some markets, aborted in others. We grant that there is a basic human urge to turn every idea that succeeds in one market into a universal truth for all markets, and that this tendency must be resisted, that such ideas, however successful in one arena, must win their way in others — and be tested again even in the one — by the same means of argument and persuasion open to all ideas. We have, however, asserted that *our* successful idea, that of basic intellectual tolerance, ought, in fact, *be* universal, and that the very fluidity and interconnectedness of idea markets mentioned above makes this an increasingly urgent goal, as the Rushdie affair demonstrates. This is not a call for cultural imperialism; to employ intolerance to enforce tolerance is not a promising approach. But it is an argument for an absolute, if paradoxical, standard for the defense of free access.

What, then, about the free access for the persistent band at Truth Missions, and the martyred racists for which they stand? Are they causing a panic in a crowded theater, in the manner of the Ayatollah? No, that won't do as an answer, even if that is their intent. It is true that we do live in a crowded theater, but the fact that the theater is becoming ever more crowded, more global, indeed, more theatrical makes it ever more important that we maintain the ability to distinguish panic from other kinds of disturbance. Everyone has the right, within the limitations of a slew of fraud and libel laws, to try to warp minds; as Ellul has demonstrated in his work on propaganda, and as our presidential elections and national advertising demonstrate in vivid prime time, warping minds seems to be a fundamental imperative of the modern state, whatever its public commitment to free inquiry.

No, McCalden and Truth Missions and their ilk have their right to try to win in our marketplace(s), along with other similarly odious and stupid ideas, and the (recast) Question Number One continues to assert itself: Just *where* can they stand to hawk their wares? Like Peattie and like Swan, they distrust the efficacy of the marketplace; they, as we, think that it suppresses all kinds of good ideas in favor of bad ones, as the first quotation above from "Trial by Jewry" demonstrates. I won't give much space to the question of the sincerity of their beliefs about Jews and the Holocaust, because, as I have already argued, I think that they, or a goodly portion of them, are sincere, and the issue is irrelevant, anyway. But they live and propagate within a sphere, a marketplace, in which certain ideas have emerged as victorious, ideas it has become their mission to attempt to universalize. A quick glance at their publications and their record of action tells most of us that in response to their sense of the larger marketplace, the world of "Boobus Northamericanus," they don't play fair, either. The booklet and the question sheet herein described are rife with lies, distortions, gaping holes in and perversions of history. For them, the only evidence of the Holocaust is some misinterpreted photographs and a vast frame-up cooked up for the Nuremberg Trials.

This lying and cheating and playing fast and loose with the truth does affect the answer to the question as to just where the Truth Missions people are free to spread their emissions—*not,* however, merely because they have been cast out of the Peattie Truth Emporium. They have not lost the *right* to peddle their goods (evils); they have, as a matter of practical fact, lost the battle of the marketplace, lost it in all the marketplaces except those, such as their own, in which local pathologies or political and cultural pressures act to render their ideas, and antisemitism in general, more palatable. For example, some of those who would do violence to Salman Rushdie would do the same to Jews for reasons that are related to one another on political and cultural levels, despite the fact that *The Satanic Verses* and Jews have nothing to do with one another in themselves. There is a great deal going on in the marketplaces of ideas that has nothing to do with the intrinsic validity, or lack thereof, of the ideas themselves.

Again, the belief that the Holocaust did not occur has, for the most part, lost the idea competition in the face of an overwhelming body of factual evidence, but despite the fact that its promoters have not lost the right to keep at their campaign, that loss puts severe practical limits on their ability to conduct it. Their books and other effusions (including a full line of cassettes!) get massively ignored, or get damning reviews from responsible historians; their revisionist academicians do not thrive in academia, not (in most cases) because they are unfairly censored, but because they perform badly or incompetently as scholars and teachers. They have trouble getting exhibit space and podium time at conferences because their ideas do not have enough appeal to those who organize conferences — or not enough appeal to overcome the negativity that their ideas inevitably inspire. This does not mean that they shouldn't ever get this exposure; an occasional debate or exhibit, with the proper counterpoint and atmosphere, would probably be found feasible, even by careful and responsible movers within the marketplace.

To quote one of the cartoon figures in "Trial by Jewry," "There were no gas chambers. If there were, *why* do you suppress the revisionists' free speech?"[2] Most conference-makers probably would answer, with Noel, that their *de facto* suppression occurs because these revisionists *do* lie and distort and make a mockery of debate. These tendencies are, however, hardly unique to these people, and an occasional well-managed debate just may have the disinfectant properties of Justice Brandeis's recommended sunlight. I recall being in an overflow crowd of Northwestern students who turned out to see American Nazi godfather figure George Lincoln Rockwell during one of his college tours in the mid-sixties. We were foolish, tasteless, insensitive for even being there — all of which qualities we students wore as merit badges, of course. We hooted, hollered, in some cases even applauded — unlike the Antioch students of whom he complained: they all turned out, but they sat and watched him in stony silence ("Sat on their hands," he said), which must have been wonderfully unnerving. In other words, we couldn't manage the social responsibility of the citizens of Antioch, but the effect of the exposure to this thinly veneered hate-monger (not long after to be murdered by one of his own) was much the same. If he made any converts that night, they were extremely quiet about it.

He did make money, of course, which may have been all he was after. Many argue that this is the real reason that the McCaldens and the Rockwells of the world should be denied a place in the marketplace, that ideas take up space, money and resources; true, many genuinely good and important ideas are being suppressed, and to spend valuable time and media and shelf space on evil ideas in the name of free access is actually to contribute to the denial of same to healthy views. But this argument is founded on a misunderstanding of how all ideas, good or bad, survive. The reason we continue to return to the tattered metaphor of the marketplace is that it does, in fact, reflect a basic reality about how ideas and information are disseminated and accepted and rejected. There is, indeed, a competition, seldom pure or fair, often inconclusive, among ideas and different versions of reality; the scene of the contest is that unitary marketplace, the human mind. Within the mind which has any claim at all to freedom and independence — and nearly all of them have at least a tiny claim — those ideas which fare best in the competition have the greatest claim to acceptance.

Yes, this is a principle more than a fact, given that most of our brains are laden with prejudices, received notions, unexamined detritus, winners of rigged competitions, but it is a principle to which all but the most thoroughly brainwashed turn when they confront reality. This means that attempts to deny the arena of competition to bad ideas, to conserve scarce resources exclusively for the high-minded, has the effect, not of suppressing those ideas, but of protecting them from the full force of competition. The messages of martyrs tend to fare well in the marketplace despite the efforts of those who bring about the martyrdom, not because those messages are intrinsically more valid than any other, but because they can compete with the advantage of association with an image that is in itself attractive, the courageous selflessness of the martyr. McCalden and Co. understand this very well. They present themselves to librarians almost exclusively as martyrs in the cause of intellectual freedom, not as purveyors of antisemitism.

So the answers to Question Number One — just what space would I give to the ideologies of hatred — and Question Number Two — just how do we carry on trade in these ideas — are, like the questions themselves, thoroughly intertwined. They are also a difficult mix of principle and practical relativity, absolutes and ambiguity. We would, we do, respond to the marketplace, granting evil its due, hoping, sometimes in vain, that the exposure and the competition itself will reduce its foothold within that marketplace.

Meanwhile, we hold to certain absolutes, based on our notion of how the mind uses, or should use, its freedom; and even here we compromise. To shift briefly to another recent and important example, intellectual freedom activists of the relatively "purist" variety confront the evil of Apartheid with a narrow, but highly significant compromise: We believe in a boycott, in rejecting all commerce with the government of South Africa — except that involving information and ideas. We believe that to stop the flow of books and other forms of communication is to censor, to hinder revolution rather than promote it. And we are opposed by social activists of a different, but also "purist" stripe, who believe that commerce is commerce, whether books or guns, and to allow such trade in information is to support the evil more than it is to reduce it. They have chosen to compromise also, in the application of the principle of intellectual freedom. These are ideas in serious conflict, in competition within the librarians' marketplace (and elsewhere — but our side claims the support of many South African antiapartheid groups, publisher groups, and both Houses of Congress). The choices involved have much more than theoretical consequences, and there is no way to settle upon a resolution that is not a mixture of principle and compromise.

It is always disappointing to bring broad, vague answers, serving up the eternal soup of absolutes and relatives, to sharp questions of practical application. But the most hard-headed responses to real questions of risk and expenditure and access must have behind them such a mixture. The most successful, the most responsive of such equations have in them the best information, and the best information is obtained by way of the broadest and freest access to all the possibilities. The practical, necessary, fundamental indivisibility of freedom asserts itself, once again, in this argument, and in the human equation.

References

1. Christopher S. Taylor, "Salman Rushdie's Insensitivity," Opinion column in *The Christian Science Monitor,* March 3, 1989, p. 18.
2. Bradley Smith, "Author, Publisher, Playwright," as quoted in "Trial by Jewry" (Manhattan Beach, Calif.: Truth Missions), p. 6.

A Bibliographic Essay

Noel Peattie

This bibliography does not attempt to cover all the entries in the bibliographical references; indeed it excludes most of them, the exceptions being titles that I invite the reader to pursue further.

There exists no bibliography of the social responsibilities movement in librarianship, but a collection of historical essays appeared under the title *Activism in American librarianship, 1962–1973,* edited by Frederick Stielow and Mary Lee Bundy (New York, Greenwood, 1987). The essays vary in quality and there are some omissions (e.g. no mention of the reform of the subject headings). For the latter one must turn to Sanford Berman's writings, especially *Prejudices and antipathies* (Metuchen, N.J., Scarecrow Press, 1971), and *Hennepin County Library cataloging bulletin* (Minnetonka, Minn., 1973–   ), as well as his comments in *Technicalities* (Armonk, N.Y., 1980–   ).

Two other periodicals which cover the social responsibilities movement are *SRRT newsletter,* available from American Library Association headquarters in Chicago, and *Interracial books for children bulletin* (New York, Council on Interracial Books for Children, 1967–   ). (The mailing address is 1841 Broadway, New York NY 10023). The *SRRT newsletter* is simply a four-to-eight-page sheet of the doings of ALA's Social Responsibilities Round Table; the newsletter had, under Berman's editorship some years back, almost the size of a small magazine. The *Interracial books for children bulletin* varies in format and scope, but confines itself almost entirely to children's books. Feature articles have discussed militarism, sexism, and stereotypes in general.

I have avoided any attempt to discuss the nature of truth in this paper, on the ground that such a discussion would take us too far from the library and into very deep waters. References to various theories of truth may be found in *Encyclopedia of philosophy* (New York, Macmillan, 1967). See also Rudolf Carnap, "Truth and confirmation," in *Readings in philosophical analysis,* selected and edited by Herbert Feigl and Wilfrid Sellars (New York, Appleton-Century-Crofts, 1949), p. 119-127. Carnap admits that "for the vast majority of statements, neither they nor their negations are confirmed or scientifically accepted" (p. 119). However, he relies on Tarski's definition of truth as basically tautological (see Alfred Tarski, "The semantic conception of truth and the foundations of semantics," in the same book, p. 52-84. Tarski gives up any attempt to arrive at a theory of truth derived from common language, and relies on a semantic definition: "a sentence is true if it is satisfied by all objects, and false otherwise" [p. 63]).

I avoided getting into definitions of truth from a humble self-awareness. I adopted the metaphor of truth as currency, and later the idea of truth as something to be lived, rather than to be defined, in order to remove the truth-question from the departments of logic and epistemology, to the department of ethics, in which I feel more comfortable.

A question which I do not take up is the creationist-scientific account of life's origins; in part because this problem has been discussed by Sanford Berman, "'In the beginning'; the creationist agenda," *Library journal,* October 15, 1985, p. 31-34. See also my coverage of the same issue, in *Sipapu,* v. 17, no. 1 (consecutive issue no. 33), p. 30-32; a discussion of the creation-science problem, with a review of William J. Bennetta's *Crusade of the credulous.*

The literature of the Holocaust is so enormous that it reduces McCalden (and other deniers) to the status of "a puny insect, shivering at a breeze." Here are four bibliographies:

Abraham J. Edelheit, *Bibliography on Holocaust literature,* Abraham J. Edelheit and Hershel Edelheit (Boulder, Colo., Westview Press, 1986). This is briefly annotated and by far the largest of the four.

The Holocaust: an annotated bibliography and resource guide, edited by David M. Szonyi (Hoboken, N.J., KTAV Publishing House for the National Jewish Resource Center, 1985) annotates every book and gives centers, museums, survivors' groups, etc.

Harry James Cargas, *The Holocaust, an annotated bibliog-*

graphy, 2d ed. (Chicago, American Library Association, 1985). Cargas, a self-styled "post–Auschwitz Catholic," has compiled this work as an act of devotion. All entries are annotated, and listed by year.

Vera Laska, *Nazism, resistance & Holocaust in World War II: a bibliography* (Metuchen, N.J., Scarecrow Press, 1985). Short, but obviously extends beyond the Holocaust.

The only extant (so far as I know) book on the neo–Nazis and "historical revisionists" is Gill Seidel, *The Holocaust denial: antisemitism, racism and the New Right* (Leeds, Beyond the Pale Collective, distributed by Turnaround Distribution, London, c1986). I wish I had read this at the beginning of this debate, since all of the arguments from the "libertarian" side are answered in the "Publisher's preface" (p. xviii–xxiii) and Michael Billig's "Introduction" (p. [xxiv]–xxx). The main text discusses Holocaust facts, interpretations, and the antisemitic right from 1945 to the present day. Seidel's book is authoritative on the subject of the New Right/neo–Nazi movement; she is correct in seeing McCalden as only the tip of a very large iceberg. (I would desire my distinguished opponent in this debate to read her book.) Her summary of Holocaust facts is excellent; her critique of "revisionist" historians is pointed; and as for McCalden, while he occupies only a few references in a very extensive treatise, his Institute for Historical Review (from which, apparently, he has since split) published a number of "revisionist" books. In any case, Seidel's book is the definitive book to thrust into the hands of "Holocaust didn't happen" skeptics. (And yes, she takes account of Romani (Gypsies), Slavic prisoners, socialists, and other groups, too; however she is mistaken when she says a revisionist conference took place at Pomona College.)

See also: Robert Singerman, *Antisemitic propaganda: an annotated bibliography and research guide;* foreword by Colin Holmes (New York, Garland, 1982) (Garland reference library of social science, v. 112). This includes a large number of ephemeral and fugitive publications.

A continuing publication which I have not seen is *Antisemitism: an annotated bibliography,* published by the Vidal Sassoon International Center for the Study of Antisemitism, the Hebrew University of Jerusalem; edited by Susan Sarah Cohen. New York, Garland, 1987–   (Garland reference library of social science, v. 366, etc.).

Five plays which explore the themes of corruption, anti-

154   *The Freedom to Lie. Peattie*

semitism, private greed, and expediency: Max Frisch, *The firebugs (Herr Biedermann und die Brandstifter); a learning-play without a lesson.* Translated by Mordecai Gorelik (New York, Hill and Wang, 1963. — Max Frisch, *Andorra,* a play in twelve scenes. Translated by Michael Bullock (New York, Hill and Wang, 1962). — Henrik Ibsen, *An enemy of the people,* ... translated and edited by James Walter McFarlane (New York, Oxford University Press, 1961). — Eugene Ionesco. *Rhinoceros & other plays.* Translated by Derek Prouse (New York, Grove Press, 1960). — Ugo Betti, *Corruption in the palace of justice* in: *The new theatre of Europe* ... an anthology edited by Robert W. Corrigan (New York, A Delta Book, 1972).

A film of Ibsen's play was produced starring Steve McQueen, and scenes from it were shown at the California Library Association conference of 1977. I objected to it on the grounds that Steve McQueen was too young, and that the drama was presented as a mere dispute between two brothers ... but the film was never released. *Rhinoceros* is most familiar to us as a film, starring the late great Zero Mostel. In the preface to *Andorra,* Frisch insists that the play has nothing to do with the little country of that name; my own suspicion is that Andorra = Austria.

On the whole question of censorship and toleration, I select James R. Bennett, *Control of information in the United States: an annotated bibliography* (Westport, Conn., Meckler, 1987); the newest volume in the long coverage of this subject. An earlier bibliography is provided by Ralph E. McCoy's *Freedom of the press, a bibliocyclopedia: ten-year supplement (1967-1977),* with a foreword by Robert B. Downs (Carbondale, Southern Illinois University Press, 1979). On pornography, the bibliographies by Betty-Carol Sellen and Patricia A. Young, *Feminists, pornography and the law: an annotated bibliography of conflict, 1970-1986* (Hamden, Conn., Shoe String Press, Library Professional Publications, 1987) and Greg Byerly, *Pornography: the conflict over sexually explicit materials in the United States* (New York, Garland, 1980) should be more than sufficient.

Versions of censorship: an anthology, edited by John McCormick and Mairi McInnes (New York, Anchor Books, 1962). This anthology does *not* include Mill, but in general supports the Millian viewpoint, which at that time was almost unchallenged among American intellectuals. Each excerpt from this book of readings is preceded by commentary, and particularly worth reading is the excerpt from Bertolt Brecht's *Galileo* (p. 66-72).

Three publications from the York University group are: *Aspects of toleration: philosophical studies,* edited by John Horton and Susan Mendus (London, Methuen, 1985); *On toleration,* edited by Susan Mendus and David Edwards (Oxford, Clarendon Press, 1987); and *Justifying toleration: conceptual and historical perspectives,* edited by Susan Mendus (Cambridge, England, Cambridge University Press, 1988). All three of these publications include discussions of toleration and the limits thereof; as one writer says, toleration is a difficult subject because it involves bringing up all sorts of unpleasant things that civilized people (the Oxford and Cambridge professors and Law Lords represented in these volumes) would prefer not to think about. Not all of the discussions are relevant to our topic, but all of them are clearly written and worth study.

Neutrality and the Berninghausen debate: David Berninghausen, then dean of the library school at the University of Minnesota, criticized social advocates in librarianship on two grounds: one, by weakening the neutrality of the profession and its institutions, they had almost destroyed their credibility; two, that a significant part of the library press had abandoned objectivity and had gone over to advocacy journalism, which Berninghausen associated with revolutionary or totalitarian societies. His two main papers aroused a batch of defenses and replies which make for some of the most interesting reading in the history of the profession. John Berry's editorial (below) accused Berninghausen of some of the same tactics he accused others of. (I stayed out of the debate, as I have my own periodical to complain in.) The library school at Minnesota is now closed, but the article on "intellectual freedom" in the *American Academic encyclopedia* is by David Berninghausen.

David Berninghausen, "Anti-thesis in librarianship: social responsibility vs. the Library Bill of Rights," *Library journal,* v. 97 (Nov. 1972), p. 3575–3681; *Library journal,* v. 97 (Dec. 1972), p. 3960–3967. Following on these two papers came the comments: "The Berninghausen debate," *Library journal,* 98 (Jan. 1973), p. 25–41; *Library journal,* 98 (May 1973), p. 1524–1529. Finally an editorial by John Berry, "Dear Dean Berninghausen," *Library journal,* 98 (Jan. 1973), p. 11.

A recent summary of social responsibility from a Canadian viewpoint is Debra Stevens, "Social responsibility and librarianship: a dilemma of professionalism," *Canadian library journal,* February 1989, 17–22. Sanford Berman mailed me this article.

An Idiosyncratic Bibliography about Freedom — Or, an Argument in the Form of a Reading List

John Swan

The brief selection which follows contains some familiar works and authors who hardly need listing in another intellectual freedom bibliography; it also contains material that could be used to make a very different argument about the relationship between freedom and its enemies. My choices were made, however, neither to summon the stamp of classic authority nor to appropriate all approaches to the problem. They are simply works which have been important — to me, at least, and in some cases to a great many others — in clarifying the nature of the issue. And yes, many of them offer eloquent support to the position that the rights of those who express hateful ideas are indissolubly linked to the rights of everyone else, that any foreclosure of debate on the grounds that some ideas are too evil to have a place in debate will neither enhance the debate nor root out the evil. The descriptions which are attached to each entry are, therefore, my personal responses much more than they are balanced summaries of the arguments.

Arendt, Hannah. "Thinking and Moral Considerations: A Lecture," in *Social Research,* 50th Anniversary Issue, vol. 51, nos. 1 and 2, Spring/Summer 1984, pp. 7–37 (originally in vol. 38, no. 3, autumn 1971).

Any discussion of the place of evil ideas, or evil itself in the idea marketplace ought to summon up this great thinker for a number of reasons, but this particular essay, a further meditation upon the insight of the "banality of evil" in her *Eichmann in Jerusalem,* has particular force because of its analysis of the nature and place of thinking itself in moral consciousness. The essay is dedicated to W.H. Auden, presumably the Auden of the chilling matter-of-factness of evil in "Musée des Beaux Arts:"

> About suffering they were never wrong,
> The Old Masters: how well they understood
> Its human position; how it takes place
> While someone else is eating or opening a window or just
> walking dully along;...
> That even the dreadful martyrdom must run its course
> Anyhow in a corner, some untidy spot
> Where the dogs go on with their doggy life and the
> torturer's horse
> Scratches its innocent behind on a tree....

Arendt's experience of Eichmann's apparent failure to do any genuine thinking, his utter reliance on cliche and prefabricated ideas, even in the shadow of the gallows, led her to ask, "Is our ability to judge, to tell right from wrong, beautiful from ugly, dependent upon our faculty of thought? Do the inability to think and a disastrous failure of what we commonly call conscience coincide?" She calls upon Socrates and Kant and the Presocratics to demonstrate that thinking itself—as distinct from the quest for knowledge or goal-oriented problem-solving—is a "dangerous and resultless enterprise," a "quest for meaning, which relentlessly dissolves and examines anew all accepted doctrines and rules" and is therefore held in deep suspicion by all the forces of convention and stability. But since our deepest problem is not with the "great villains," but instead with "the nonwicked everybody who has no special motives and for this reason is capable of *infinite* evil," thinking becomes essential because it forces the examination of action, moral and political and otherwise, and thus awakens the faculty of judgment—especially necessary "when everybody is swept away unthinkingly by what everybody else does and believes in." For me this is a perspective which is particularly relevant to the efficacy of free and open dialogue.

Chevigny, Paul. *More Speech: Dialogue Rights and Modern Liberty.* Philadelphia: Temple University Press, 1988.

This new study of an old issue is important for several reasons. It provides a lucid (and critical) synthesis of the strongest lines of libertarian defense of free speech (from Mill to Thomas Emerson and Thomas Scanlon), along with healthy doses of theory from a considerable range of relevant theorists (Freud and Lacan, Lawrence Kohlberg and Carol Gilligan, Marcuse, Chomsky, Habermas...). More particularly, it is a remarkably ambitious and successful attempt to provide an argument for open dialogue that transcends the cultural assumptions of Western individuality and even traditional rationalism "intended to show that systematic limits on dialogue have effects on understanding, on problem-solving, and on the legitimacy of the government." Chevigny projects a vision of freedom "rooted in the social nature of language" that puts many of the above theorists to work in a thesis of real power and originality. The use to which I put him is evident in my first essay.

Ellul, Jacques. *Propaganda: The Formation of Men's Attitudes,* translated by Konrad Kellen and Jean Lerner. New York: Knopf, 1966 (originally published in 1962 as *Propagandes*).

This pioneering and controversial analysis of the nature and workings of propaganda has long since proven itself to be a powerful predictor of human behavior in our propaganda-soaked world, but it is particularly telling in this context because of Ellul's understanding of the relationship between propaganda and information. It is no longer sufficient to distinguish the two by describing the former as "irrational," appealing to the passions, and the latter as furnishing "facts" and appealing to reason. Because the state and the corporation require loyalty and patronage and "modern man needs a relation to facts, a self-justification to convince himself that by acting in a certain way he is obeying reason and proved experience," in our age of mass media "propaganda's content increasingly resembles information."

The debate surrounding the freedom of information should be informed by Ellul's crucial insight about the net effect of information in the massive doses we experience: "A surfeit of data, far from permitting people to make judgments and form opinions, prevents them from doing so and actually paralyzes them.... The mechanisms of modern information induce a sort of hypnosis in the individual, who cannot get out of the field that has been laid out for him by the information.... The more the techniques of distributing information develop, the more the individual is shaped by such information." This is not, of course, an argument for less information, but a warning that we must examine our relationship to this "rational propaganda" which, according to Ellul, is depriving humans of themselves, of their capability for genuine thinking (*vide* Arendt).

Foskett, D.J. *The Creed of a Librarian—No Politics, No Religion, No Morals.* London: The Library Association, 1962. (Reference, Special and Information Section, North Western Group, Occasional Papers No. 3.)

The title of this eloquent paper is somewhat misleading in our particular context. It is, in fact, an argument *for* a positive philosophy of librarianship and a criticism of the prevailing lack thereof (still true a quarter of a century later, unless you are satisfied with the ubiquitous platitudes about service that would suit a hamburger stand as well as a library). Indeed, he sets forth the outlines of a philosophy in which advocacy is at least as prominent as libertarian access: "As librarians, we are the guardians—not the owners, but the guardians—of knowledge. If we have a contribution to make to the progress of our civilization, then we must seek after the truth, because this is what prevails and ensures that civilization does progress. On the other hand, . . . who are we to decide what people shall read, who are librarians that they set themselves up as censors?" For Foskett, the development of a genuine understanding of librarianship as a "social process" will help us resolve the dilemma between "the quest for truth and the desire for absolute freedom." Librarians may not have the censor's right, but "we do have the right of our office, the right to decide what shall be in our libraries and what shall not." Although his emphasis ought to make us defenders of open access uncomfortable—"we grant the conductor of a symphony orchestra the right not to play the latest popular songs"—his essential argument is most relevant. The negatives in his title—lifted, the author tells us, from a lecture by J.D. Cowley—refer to the essential neutrality of the service role: "During reference service, the librarian ought virtually to vanish as an individual person, except in so far as his personality sheds light on the working of the library. He must be the reader's *alter ego,* immersed in his politics, his religion, his morals." This is an ideal, of course, perhaps in need of a good deal of qualification, but it is a strong statement of the democratic version of the librarian's mission.

Geller, Evelyn. *Forbidden Books in American Public Libraries,*

1876-1939: A Study in Cultural Change. Westport, Conn.: Greenwood Press, 1984.

This survey, a sociological analysis and a cultural history, ought to be required background reading for anyone exploring the role of censorship in American librarianship. It contains a wealth of information about the ideals and the assumptions, both democratic and elitist, that went into the origins of the public library movement, as well as the policies and actions of the political and cultural leaders thereof. Over the course of that movement, Geller discerns a basic shift: "When the first large public libraries were established, free educational institutions were seen as guardians against religious and class discrimination. The knowledge relevant to their goals was certified and useful knowledge, while policies of neutrality through exclusion, mirroring the separation of church and state, respected strong religious identifications. These functions of the library were compatible with censorship. At the end of this study political identities were paramount, free education had been taken on by other institutions, and education on political issues and mass media propaganda had become an important function." The transformation from guardian of the highest ideals of democratic culture to facilitator of democratic access was neither simple nor smooth, and there is much more involved than a shift from censor to champion of freedom of access—neither end of the trend can be fairly summarized so simply. But the sometimes odd contours of the present role of public libraries, both as institutions of freedom and as preservers of what is in reality a quite constricted *status quo,* are much illuminated by this important book.

Haiman, Franklyn S. *Speech and Law in a Free Society.* Chicago: University of Chicago Press, 1981.

This multiple-award-winning study of communication and its social and legal ramifications is founded upon certain premises, among which are the following: "Social order is a means to maximizing individual liberty and security. It is not an end in itself. . . . Symbolic behavior . . . lies at the core of a free society. . . . Whether or not one believes, theoretically, in the existence of absolute truth, a democracy presumes that we can never be certain it has been attained by any fallible human being. Thus reliance is placed on a free marketplace of ideas trusting that, even if the wisest decisions do not always emerge victorious, the likelihood is greater of approximating truth and avoiding the most serious errors when communication is free than when it is restricted." This forthright belief in the efficacy of the contest between ideas is applied to many different situations, ranging through many of the thorniest free speech issues (defamation of individuals and groups, invasion of privacy, lies, intimidation, illegal incitement, government secrecy), always with sensitivity to the practical and theoretical problems — and to the fact that the contest is not seldom a rigged affair. In the area of the promulgation of lies and misrepresentations, Haiman reminds us that "particularly in the realm of religion or of public and social policy, where empirical questions are almost inseparable from inference and interpretation, there is the danger that authoritative attempts to say what is or is not 'true' would lead to the establishment of orthodoxies and heresies that have no place in a democratic society." He refers repeatedly and usefully to Justice Brandeis's classic admonition that "if there be time to expose through discussion the falsehood and fallacies . . . the remedy to be applied is more speech, not enforced silence."

Hamilton, Richard. *Who Voted for Hitler?* Princeton, N.J.: Princeton University Press, 1982.

I include this work (out of a number of probing analyses of the political and psychological roots of Nazi power) because it is a thoroughgoing examination of the environment and the voting behavior of a group of people at a point when they were still citizens of a democracy — troubled and under many and various pressures, to be sure — responding as individuals to the broad spectrum of political communication. That is, when Hitler's party took 37.3 percent of the vote in the national elections of July 31, 1932, they acquired a position in German political life that set the stage for the disasters to come, and they acquired it, not through the coercion that would assure later electoral success, but by convincing three out of every eight voters that the Nazis offered them the best hope for the future. Hamilton carefully and convincingly dismantles the most familiar explanation, that Hitler built his base among the disgruntled and struggling lower middle class, by demonstrating his strong appeal among important segments of upper-class voters and in many other groups. Far from spreading evil with a calculated repertory of standard lies, the Nazi politicians appealed to each group in its own terms, according to its own hopes and illusions. This excellent study provides a reminder that evil can be communicated, in the right circumstances, by the same means and often in the same words as any other kind of message. Exorcising evil by isolating the words which are its medium is itself an illusion.

Hauptman, Robert. *Ethical Challenges in Librarianship.* Phoenix, Ariz.: Oryx Press, 1988.

Hauptman, one of the very few who have explored the ethical and moral ramifications of librarianship with any sustained seriousness, was the perpetrator of the famous "bomb" experiment (recounted in his much-quoted article, "Professionalism or Culpability? An Experiment in Ethics," *Wilson Library Bulletin,* vol. 50, no. 8, April 1976, pp. 626–27) in which he posed as a shaggy revolutionary type and went to a series of reference desks asking for information about the building of an explosive device powerful enough to blow up a small house. His criticism of the librarians who sought to comply without questioning the question (and that included virtually all of them) has itself spawned a lot of criticism (see Swan below, for instance), but his continued insistence that librarians be aware of the moral dimension of their information-dispensing role has been a very valuable addition to the literature. The work at hand is illuminated by this same insistence, covering every area of library activity (the first book in the literature to do so), and related areas, such as information brokerage, consulting, and expanding computer applications. In his chapter on censorship, Hauptman addresses the issues raised by Swan and Peattie specifically, as well as others in which the imperatives of free access and social responsibility seem to be, at least in part, in opposition. In this and in a good deal else he provides much that is thoughtful and useful.

Hentoff, Nat. *The First Freedom: The Tumultuous History of Free Speech in America.* New York: Delacorte Press, 1980.

Hentoff has long been one of America's most vocal and most effective activists for intellectual freedom. This work is written very much from the perspective of the uncompromising champion of free speech although he gives full play to the ambiguities, the defeats and the divisions that have characterized this history—including the much-echoed assertion of one justice that "the First Amendment is not a suicide pact." His closing coverage of the bitter and protracted Nazis-and-the-ACLU vs. Skokie-and-most-of-the-rest-of-the-world fight is alone worth the price of admission. And worth quoting from that text is ACLU Director Aryeh Neier's statement: "As a Jew, and a refugee from Nazi Germany, I have strong personal reasons for finding the Nazis repugnant. Freedom of speech protects my right to denounce Nazis with all the vehemence I think proper. Despite my hatred of their vicious doctrine, I realize that it is in my interests to defend their right to preach it."

Milgram, Stanley. *Obedience to Authority; An Experimental View.* New York: Harper and Row, 1974.

Like the Hamilton book, and also like the Arendt essay, this famous account of a controversial experiment in social psychology finds a place in this list because of the insight it offers as to what forces lead people who are otherwise "normal" to interpret information and act upon it to evil ends. Milgram specifically confronted the phenomenon of obedience, "the psychological mechanism that links individual action to political purpose . . . the dispositional cement that binds men to systems of authority." Recognizing that the Nazi policies of extermination "could only have been carried out on a massive scale if a very large number of people obeyed orders," the author designed an experiment to measure the capacity for obedience, or in the given context, measure "how far the participant will comply with the experimenter's instructions before refusing to carry out the actions required of him." The shocking result of the experiment, confirmed repeatedly with different samplings of "ordinary people," with varied parameters, was that the majority of us are only too willing to obey under the proper conditions of freely accepted authority, even when we believe that in obeying we are doing harm — and in some cases even killing — another human being. Milgram's theory of "agency," by which we abdicate our moral individuality and put ourselves in the hands of a higher authority, has powerful ramifications in many areas of social behavior, of course. For the sake of the present argument, it suggests that people are not led to do evil merely by hearing exhortations to do so in the marketplace of ideas; they must first be led to surrender their place as free consumers in that market.

Mill, John Stuart. *On Liberty.* In *Three Essays,* with an introduction by Richard Wollheim. Oxford: Oxford University Press, 1975. (Merely one convenient edition of this essay, which first appeared independently in 1859.)

"Human beings owe to each other help to distinguish the better from the worse, and encouragement to choose the former and avoid the latter. . . . But neither one person, nor any number of persons, is warranted in saying to another human creature of ripe years, that he shall not do with his life for his own benefit what he chooses to do with it. . . . Considerations to aid his judgement, exhortations to strengthen his will, may be offered to him, even obtruded on him . . . but he himself is the final judge. All errors which he is likely to commit against advice and warning, are far outweighed by the evil of allowing others to constrain him to what they deem his good." For all the years of criticism, rereading, readjustment to which the Millian doctrine of individuality and freedom has been subjected, it remains the *locus classicus* of modern libertarian argument. We may not rise so readily to his ringing faith, but we hear the music — as in his defense of the Mormons (regarded by many as the embodiment of evil in his day, and personally disapproved of by Mill himself): "If civilization has got the better of barbarism when barbarism had the world to itself, it is too much to profess to be afraid lest barbarism, after having been fairly got under, should revive and conquer civilization. A civilization that can thus succumb to its vanquished enemy, must first have become so degenerate, that neither its appointed priests and teachers, nor anybody else, has the capacity . . . to stand up for it. If this be so, the sooner such a civilization receives notice to quit, the better."

Moon, Eric. *Book Selection and Censorship in the Sixties*. New York: Bowker, 1969.

This generous compilation of *Library Journal* pieces from a fractious and significant time is cited here only as a general (and unnecessary) reminder that the library profession and the American Library Association have crafted, struggled with, and defended a philosophy of intellectual freedom of striking purity which they have supported and developed with consistency and often applied to the real world to remarkably good effect. (The one official document that most clearly mirrors this collective achievement is the ALA *Intellectual Freedom Manual*.) This is due in no small part to a courageous and committed band of leaders who (whether or not they have been comfortable with one another) have collectively fought the good fight. Some obvious names are John Philip Immroth, Eli Oboler, Dorothy Broderick, Judith Krug, E.J. Josey, and Gerald Shields, just to name a few who have left a significant paper trail, but for this entry Eric Moon is the most natural choice. This anthology is a convenient portrait of the aforementioned good fight, but many other essays and columns by him are also relevant (for instance, the rare combination of wit and moral vision in the address, "Association Agonies: Life with ALA," printed in the February 1972 *American Libraries* and in Bill Katz's *Library Lit. 3 — the Best of 1972*). No one has brought more patient, eloquent courage to writing about and fighting for genuine freedom of access for all librarians and all their patrons and all their points of view, than Eric Moon.

Mura, David. *A Male Grief: Notes on Pornography and Addiction.* Minneapolis: Milkweed Editions, 1987. (Originally published in vol. 6, no. 2, spring 1985, of *Milkweed Chronicle.*)

"There are certain states of mind that the closer one understands them, the closer one comes to experiencing evil." In terms of its literal argument, this brief, searing meditation on pornography "used as a drug, a way of numbing psychic pain" does not belong in a list summoned to support a libertarian position. It rejects the position that pornography is just another form of speech (however aberrant) to be protected. "The ultimate example of capitalism," pornography is the most virulent expression of our collective compulsion, "our endless consumption of images." But the essay (the awareness, and the copy, of which I owe to the poet Tam Lin Neville) is included here because of its unparalleled power in tracing the etiology of its author's addiction to a form of expression that robs both classes of victim, the women exploited by it and the compulsive consumer, of their humanity. For those of us who do believe that it is impossible effectively to define and excise the expression of evil, including pornography, from the spectrum of speech without endangering all freedom of expression, this essay helps us understand the full implications of our position. It is simply not enough to dismiss the antipornographers as repressed suppressors of speech. The speech we defend does include expression that is symptomatic of genuine evil. Mura, a gifted poet as well as essayist, gives perhaps the most tellingly intimate account of the effect of the evil on its consumer. Mention certainly ought to be made of at least two of the better-known figures who have analyzed the evil and the male-dominated culture which breeds it from the point of view of its victims, Susan Griffin (see "Pornography and Silence" and other essays in *Made from This Earth: An Anthology of Writings by Susan Griffin,* Harper and Row, 1982) and Adrienne Rich (*On Lies, Secrets, and Silence: Selected Prose, 1966–1978,* W.W. Norton, 1979).

Rushdie, Salman. "The Book Burning," *The New York Review of Books,* March 2, 1989, p. 26.

Rushdie wrote this in January, before the Ayatollah Khomeini put a price on his head, in response to the early furor over the publication of his novel *The Satanic Verses,* which took the form of protests and book-burnings in areas in England with large Muslim populations. Although he did not yet know that his book would be the center of a major international political controversy, and that perhaps his whole life would have to be spent in hiding, his reaction to the public burning in Bradford, West Yorkshire, shows a vivid awareness of what is at stake. This is not the place for a consideration of the cultural, religious, and political issues surrounding this unprecedented form of terrorism; however, Rushdie's brief article and the events which occasioned it, and followed it, does deserve a place here.

Whatever else the *Satanic Verses* incident involves, it is centered upon the reaction of True Believers to what they regard as blasphemous, hurtful untruth. In Rushdie's words, "a powerful tribe of clerics has taken over Islam. These are the contemporary Thought Police. They have turned Muhammad into a perfect being, his life into a perfect life, his revelation into the unambiguous, clear event it originally was not. Powerful taboos have been erected. One may not discuss Muhammad as if he were human, with human virtues and weaknesses. One may not discuss the growth of Islam as a historical phenomenon, as an ideology born out of its time." Rushdie asserts that "in this War of the Word, the guardians of religious truth have been telling their followers a number of lies." He defends his work against the charges of blasphemy with skill and cogency; but of course, those who would eradicate both him and his book do not read *The New York Review of Books*—have not, for the most part, even read *The Satanic Verses*. Rushdie reminds us, "How fragile civilization is; how merrily a book burns!" And his experience reminds us of the perils attendant upon the conviction that possession of the Truth confers the power to punish those who transgress against it.

Scanlon, T.M., Jr. "Freedom of Expression and Categories of Expression," in David Copp and Susan Wendell, eds., *Pornography and Censorship.* Buffalo, N.Y.: Prometheus Books, 1983. (Originally in *University of Pittsburgh Law Review,* vol. 40, no. 4, summer 1979.)

This is just one of many lucid exegeses of the issues surrounding free communication, its generators and its audience, by this leading legal scholar. "Rights purport to place limits on what individuals or the state may do, and the sacrifices they entail are in some cases significant." Scanlon approaches the problem of the allocation of rights, the old problem of balance, by way of a very general group of categories: "the interests of participants, the interests of audiences, and the interests of bystanders." The clarity of his perspective allows him to weigh the benefits and costs of both censoring and permitting the communication of potentially harmful defamatory or pornographic material in some very difficult and ambiguous situations. He concludes ruefully that "the costs that audiences and bystanders are required to bear in order to provide for free political debate are generally quite high." High, but, as he finally asserts, necessary.

Swan, John C. "Minimum Qualifications and Intellectual Freedom," *Library Journal,* vol. 106, no. 15, September 1, 1981, pp. 1595–99.

_____. "Ethics at the Reference Desk: Comfortable Theories and Tricky Practices," in *The Reference Librarian,* no. 4, pp. 99–116 (issue also published as a monograph, *Ethics and Reference Services,* ed. by Bill Katz and Ruth Fraley. New York: Haworth Press, 1982).

_____. "Mad Bombers and Ethical Librarians: A Dialogue with Robert Hauptman and John Swan," co-authored with Robert Hauptman. *Catholic Library World,* vol. 58, no. 4 (Jan./Feb. 1987), pp. 161–63 (an installment of Paul Wiener's "On My Mind" column).

We who cite ourselves a lot are pathetic, insecure beings, but these three selections ought to be listed because of their relevance to the debate at hand. The first is included as a response to the Peattie tendency to characterize the "neutrality" of civil libertarian librarians as a valueless limbo. We have, in fact, often regarded our roles as interactive and dynamic. Indeed, for many of us, the *refusal* to share the perspectives on controversial issues that we acquire as professionals and as consumers of the media in our charge can be regarded as a failure to live up to the highest standards of service. There are a number of difficulties and a genuine paradox in this position, it should be admitted, and this article is an attempt to explore them. My basic argument is that "the librarian is an educator, not a passive instrument of information processing," and "it is possible, therefore, to accept both the civil libertarian view that library material should never be suppressed ... and the belief that the librarian should be free to share his knowledge and judgment of the material." That this is a position not of neutrality but of positive advocacy is emphasized in the other two pieces cited, the first of which has a passage taking issue with Robert Hauptman's conclusions from his "bomb" experiment (see Hauptman, above) and the second of which is a debate over points raised in that article (more of a discussion, in which we discover much common ground, not unlike the "debate" that has prompted this book). Quoting myself, again, from *The Reference Librarian:* "It is simply not the case that the reference librarian makes 'no ethical judgment,' when her/his role is founded on a belief in the profound ethical value of freedom of information." And from the latter debate: "Librarians who withhold information out of disapproval of the possible uses of that information are merely violating one ethical construct in favor of what they misconstrue to be a competing one." Hauptman's closing salvo makes clear that this argument/exploration is indeed relevant to the present debate in its engagement with the question of evil: "I continue to insist that it is mandatory to consider our individual actions within an ethical context, and to give a considered response. Stanley Milgram's *Obedience to Authority* makes it unequivocally clear to me that we must guard against being seduced into . . . abetting unethical activity." Granted — given the difficulty of knowing just when freedom of access abets, rather than exposes, such activity.

Epilogue on the Problem of Seeing Evil in What One Reads, Written after a Local School Board Meeting:

David Budbill is an award-winning Vermont novelist and playwright. His 1978 young people's book, *Bones on Black Spruce Mountain* (now a Bantam/Skylark paperback), is a tough-minded, positive, informative (where else in fiction can you get the exact contents of two backpacks necessary for an extended mountain trek?) tale of mystery, challenge, and self-discovery. It garnered a clutch of excellent reviews from leading publications in and out of the field of young people's literature, as well as the Dorothy Canfield Fisher Award. It also harbors a few passages containing language not usually found in books read by fourth or fifth graders — a very occasional "hell," "damn," and "shit," and a brief amused (and amusing) reminiscence of urinating on someone's prized flowers. This was enough to transform the book into "garbage" for a group of local parents and their supporters, who fervently believe that the appearance of this "filth" in a book for young people legitimizes it and causes them to go and do likewise. This is, of course, a very common belief, and if simplistic, not altogether in error: we all agree that reading can be a dangerous activity.

But for most of us, including, fortunately, the entire school board at this particular meeting, the good of this particular book so thoroughly outweighed the possible harm that the censors failed, despite a good deal of diplomacy, then heat and anger, to carry their point. This was in part because the child of the originally outraged parents had not been forced to read this particular book, had been given other options, and a series of carefully prepared policies had been followed to allow for reasonable parental control — of their own child's reading, not anyone else's children's reading. The fact that the group in question still protested the presence of the book in the library and as a "free reading" choice in the classroom was therefore seen as an attempt to abrogate the rights of others by the board and many others in that packed room. In other words, it may well be that many in that room who were against the attempt at censorship still believed that the "bad words" were at best a necessary evil, rather than part of the living fabric of a realistic fiction.

The point of inserting this event here, a common one, of course — and no doubt to be played out again in our own small community, because the losers were an angry lot who felt that they had been done in once again by a bunch of "liberals" — is not to crow about one more small victory for freedom. It is rather to make the point that there is demonstrated in this small, emotional confrontation an enormous difficulty standing in the way of anyone who would suppress the speaking of evil and thereby improve the moral atmosphere. The earnest folk who protested the use of David Budbill's book see evil in it; the words they used on the evening of the school board meeting made that very clear. And even among its defenders were many who saw, and forgave, elements of evil in it. Those of us for whom profanity (and much "worse," it is unnecessary to say) is an exceptable and inevitable element in the tissue of modern prose are not likely to classify it as "evil" at all. Our sense of "evil" has a great deal more to do with Nazis and genocide and racism, and we are impatient and distrustful of those who worry more about mere words, and would shield their — and our — children from the language of harsh reality.

The old, simple question remains: whose evil are we going to clean up, whose sense of morality are we going to rig the game for? It is not enough to assume that on some basic level they all converge — even in the unlikely event that they do — because in terms of all the practical, quotidian levels of political and philosophical communication, they do not. We can, we must, put the majority of our resources into promoting good and discouraging evil, but it is always necessary to remember that there is precious little consensus as to the particulars of which is which.

This is the reason for the communication device, as homely and flawed as it is, which we refer to as democracy. We saw it in free-wheeling action that night at the school board. The losers saw it as a device which failed to support the truth, and we who usually find ourselves on the losing side of national politics often share that view. But as long as the basic unit of collective decision-making remains the individual, as blindered and semi-conscious as the creature is, it is the necessary device, and it can only function well with as broad a spectrum of expression, good and evil, as we can tolerate. The human imagination demands no less.

Index